Modern Miniature
Daffodils

Modern Miniature Daffodils

SPECIES AND HYBRIDS

by
James S. Wells

Foreword by Christopher D. Brickell
Drawings by Michael Salmon

B. T. Batsford Ltd • London

THIS BOOK IS DEDICATED
IN GRATITUDE TO
ALEC GRAY
THE MAN WHO STARTED IT ALL.

© 1989 by Timber Press, Inc.

First published 1989

ISBN 0 7134 6456 9

Printed in Hong Kong
for the publisher

B. T. Batsford Ltd
4 Fitzhardinge Street
London W1H 0AH

Contents

Foreword

In an era when a plethora of gardening books of varying merit and quality tumble like so much confetti from the publishers' presses it is a very great pleasure to be asked to provide a foreword for Jim Wells' authoritative book on modern miniature daffodils.

Many modern gardening books are written by authors with little practical knowledge of the art and craft of the profession. It will be evident to the reader that this book has been "crafted" by an author who not only has a deep theoretical understanding of his subject, but also has an intimate practical knowledge of growing miniature daffodils. It is a book written from personal experience in a very readable fashion with meticulous attention to detail and critical appraisal and discussion of all the miniature daffodils described.

In a way this is perhaps not surprising as Jim Wells' professional career in plant propagation demanded similar care and attention to detail as may be seen from his excellent book *Plant Propagation Practices* first published in 1955 and recently revised.

The last book of note on miniature daffodils was written by Alec Gray, a doyen of the *Narcissus* world some 30 years ago. It was the standard of its day and until the publication of this present book has remained unequalled. Jim Wells, however, has provided all bulb enthusiasts with an up-to-date work on his subject which is undoubtedly a worthy successor and likely to remain a standard for as long, if not longer, than its predecessor.

It is not, however, simply a book for the enthusiast. It will certainly be greatly valued by them but it is also a book to stimulate interest and encourage even those with very limited knowledge of growing dwarf bulbs into attempting to cultivate and to enjoy, with only reasonable care, the charm of the many delightful miniature daffodils available today. Most are ideal bulbs to grow in pots, pans or other containers for those without (or of course with) gardens; others increase happily and give pleasure annually in the rock garden; and a few challenge the skills of the expert grower.

All these are covered in this most readable and informative account which distils the author's wealth of knowledge and practical experience to provide a book of value to the beginner and expert alike.

Christopher D. Brickell

Alec Gray, who first saw the beauty in miniature daffodils.

John Blanchard who is now
producing exciting miniatures of
exceptional quality.

Introduction

It is now more than 30 years since that excellent book *Miniature Daffodils,* written by the dean of miniatures, Alec Gray, was published. These years have seen substantial changes in first, the nomenclature of the many subspecies and varieties, and second, in the complete acceptance of a wide range of miniature hybrids, named and grown with pleasure, in almost every division of the genus. Now, as then, there are no readily available miniatures in the *Poeticus* division—although I have heard that some have been bred and are being tested. In every other respect the advances have been substantial, with many fine hybrids coming into general acceptance and use. Both taxonomy and the nomenclature have been greatly altered, culminating in the recent publication of the *Flora Europaea* in which the genus Narcissus is substantially condensed. As a result, names which have been current for years have been swallowed up into larger groups with little or no differentiation. This 'lumping' as contrasted with 'splitting' previously common may not meet with universal approval, for change, no matter how minor, is bound to upset someone. In the interest of clear communication I have incorporated the changes endorsed by *Flora Europaea* but have also noted references to early literature.

The *European Garden Flora* was published in 1986 and in this the changes suggested are less drastic. However, I now understand that in the new daffodil register being prepared by the Royal Horticultural Society, recent name changes may be largely ignored and the basis of the new checklist will be the scheme as outlined in 1968 by Fernandes, published in the R.H.S. Daffodil Yearbook of that year. This will greatly simplify matters for the only changes proposed to Fernandes as we go to print are as follows:

N. barlae. Not recognized by any modern author. This will be merged in *N. tazetta* subsp. *pannizianus.*

N. × dubius will be treated as *N. dubius.*

The following additional taxa will be recognized:

N. canariensis (Canary Islands)

N. elegans var. *oxypetalus* (N. Africa)

N. atlanticus (Morocco)

N. capax (N.W. France)

Apart from these botanical matters there has also been a substantial increase in the number of excellent hybrids, produced by keen growers in all parts of the world, and especially in North America. This interest in miniatures can be directly attributed to the American Daffodil Society, which was the first international group to attempt to define what is meant by a miniature and to produce a list of "approved" hybrids and species. This list, a living and vital list, is continually examined and updated by deletions and additions as seem appropriate, so that all interested growers have an immediate guide to those bulbs considered to be in the miniature category. The list has, without doubt, done much to awaken interest in these charming plants, and will continue to do so in the future.

I have been most fortunate in obtaining details of more than 100 species recorded by Alec Gray when he was actively collecting and growing. This information has been used selectively where necessary, supplemented by my own observations in growing and attempting to sort out some of the variations. Many bulbs available under identical names can vary greatly. This has come about, I presume, because of multiple collections from slightly different plants in the wild, some of which have proven to be much more desirable than others. Superior forms of most of the species are available, and where possible I have tried to indicate these differences.

The list of hybrids is substantial, so some selection had to be made. I have confined my descriptions to those which are clearly desirable and outstanding, and wherever possible, available. In most instances I have grown the bulb for at least a year, unless otherwise noted. Some may not be immediately available from local retailers, but most can be obtained either by purchase or barter, if the reader will take the trouble to search out and contact similar enthusiasts around the world. But I agree that finding some requires considerable tenacity and persuasiveness, as well as a generous sharing of those bulbs which you may already have. I have found that the miniature daffodil community is a highly specialized group of keen enthusiasts who are, in the main, more than ready to exchange ideas, information, and bulbs. That is how I started, and the collection I now have is a monument to the generosity of many people. They know who they are, and to each and every one I say again, "Thank you."

Section One
Culture

CHAPTER ONE

What Is A Miniature Daffodil?

Both the Royal Horticultural Society in England and the American Daffodil Society have undertaken to define the meaning of 'miniature.' Neither definition is entirely adequate, and because of the wide diversity of both plants and growing conditions, particularly in North America, I doubt that a really accurate and working definition can be formulated. The R. H. S., in an attempt to be both simple and brief, requires that the flower, when open and spread-out, should measure no more than 2 in. (5 cm) in diameter. By this definition a number of bulbs with rather large flowers could be considered miniature when the more appropriate description is 'dwarf' or 'short stem.'

The committee appointed in North America to consider the problem was requested to take into account those bulbs which over a period appeared to be true miniatures in all areas and under all conditions. The committee concluded that due to the wide diversity in seasonal conditions as well as growing areas, plants could vary so greatly from year to year that several criteria were required. Those which they established are:

1. The plant must be suitable for the small rock garden.
2. It must not be acceptable for exhibition in a standard class.
3. It must conform to the general characteristics of those bulbs which clearly belong in the miniature class, without argument or discussion.
4. The bulb should be commercially available.

Using these yardsticks the committee produced an initial list, which was eventually adopted by the Society as the Approved List.

In April 1987 these rules were amended as follows, to make it easier for new hybrids to be shown and considered for possible approval.

1. Miniature Candidate: Any named or numbered "small" daffodil may be considered a "Miniature "Candidate."
2. The status "Miniature Candidate" can exist indefinitely.
3. Such candidates can be shown at A. D. S. shows by the originator and others and are eligible for A. D. S. awards in the miniature section.
4. Final approval to the A. D. S. Approved List shall require the recommendation of five growers instead of three.
5. As an integral part of the recommendation, each sponsor must complete a simple, comprehensive form, outlining performance characteristics as the candidate grows under

their conditions. A photograph of the foliage and flower of the Miniature Candidate must be submitted with the application for approval to miniature status.

6. It is no longer necessary for the bulb to be "commercially available."

In 1978 the A. D. S. worked out procedures now formulated into *Ground Rules for Miniature Daffodils,* which govern the display and judging of these bulbs. Very occasionally bulbs which have been on the list for some time are dropped when careful consideration suggests that the bulb should not be included in the list.

With this degree of thoughtful care, the Approved List has become a valuable guide to would-be growers, confident that the bulbs listed will conform to the established standards. Inevitably, there are bulbs which do not fall neatly into any category: should there be an intermediate class for these? This idea has not met with universal approval, although it is once again being considered by a committee. These fine distinctions did not bother Alec Gray, for in his book *Miniature Daffodils* he lists a number of both species and cultivars which would not be accepted under modern rules. *N. pseudonarcissus* subsp. *obvallaris* is a typical example as is the cultivar 'February Gold.' So although both are listed by Gray they cannot be included in this book under the current American standards, although they would be in England. Happily there are more than enough good bulbs which can be included, so the omission of some of the old standbys need not be mourned.

Among the species as a whole there are many forms which just naturally fit into our conception of a real miniature. There are a number of excellent bulbs in both the *Pseudonarcissus* (or Trumpet) Section and in the *Tazetta* Section which just are not miniatures and so have to be omitted. But we do have a group of miniature species, with representatives in most of the main botanical divisions which fall naturally into the miniature category. The divisions to which a hybrid belongs is determined by the general appearance and effect of the bloom. Thus, hybrids which clearly display characteristics of *N. cyclamineus* are placed in the same division as the species *N. cyclamineus*—Division 6.

This brings us to the point where we should consider a more detailed outline of the botany and botanical divisions into which the genus *Narcissus* has been divided. This is necessary because there have been many changes in the nomenclature of these bulbs in recent years, to the point that it is sometimes difficult to be accurate when discussing and ordering a bulb that is being sought. *Flora Europaea* 1980 proposed a number of sweeping changes whereby many of the subspecies previously recognized and named are now merged under one name. This is particularly true in *N. bulbocodium* and *N. triandrus,* in both of which were many named forms previously grown as subspecies because the cultivated plants can be quite clearly differentiated.

Other changes have come about due to the rule of priority of publication. If a plant was described perhaps 100 years ago under a certain name which never came into general use, that name if validly published, takes precedence over any other name applied later, even if the latter is well known and in constant use. As an example, the large-flowered form of *N. triandrus,* native to the Isles of Glenans off the coast of Brittany, was known in cultivation as *N. triandrus calathinus.* The name was subsequently changed to *N. triandrus* var. *loiseleurii,* and just as we gardeners had become used to that and managed to pronounce it more or less correctly, we are told by *Flora Europaea* that the earliest valid, and therefore correct, name should now be *N. triandrus* subsp. *capax.* I hope this example will demonstrate that a

Narcissus bulbocodium subsp. *bulbocodium* var. *filifolius*. An excellent example of a typical miniature daffodil.

modest amount of current botanical thinking may make it easier to understand the problem.

The genus *Narcissus* is part of the larger botanical family AMARYLLI-DACAEA which in turn encompasses some 85 genera and over 1100 species, mostly bulbous. The genus is divided into 9 sections, separating the different forms such as the trumpet daffodils (*Pseudonarcissus*), the jonquils (*Jonquillae*), and others. Not all of these sections will interest us in our pursuit of miniatures.

Section 1, 2 and 3

Sections #1, #2, and #3 are concerned entirely with the fall blooming bulbs *N. humilis, N. serotinus* and *N. broussonetti,* all of which are collectors items only.

Section 4

Section #4, *Tazettae* contains only one or two miniature types. *N. italicus* must now include a bulb which we have grown as *N. canaliculatus* and is now known as *N. italicus* var. *lacticolor*.

Section 5

Section #5 *Narcissus*. There are no natural miniatures in this section, nor have any dwarf hybrids been produced so far.

Section 6

Section #6 *Jonquillae*. There are some changes here. The most obvious is the change of *N. juncifolius* to *N. requienii* or possibly to *N. assoanus*, while another bulb which we do grow and enjoy under the name *N. henriquesii* is not mentioned. The plant previously known as *N. rupicola* subsp. *pedunculatus* has now become a species with the name *N. cuatrecasasii*, but as this name is relatively new and does not conform to Fernandes, it may not be recognized.

Section 7

Section #7 Ganymedes or Triandrus. Here there has been considerable lumping. The basic species is now *N. triandrus*. The first subspecies is *N. triandrus* subsp. *pallidulus* which is to include such bulbs previously known as *N. triandrus* var. *concolor*, *N. triandrus* var. *pulchellus* and *N. triandrus* var. *cernuus*, these all being considered as but minor variations of the form to be "lumped" under subsp. *pallidulus*. Also included is *N. triandrus* var. *aurantiacus*, which in my opinion clearly deserves at least a sub specific rank in its own right. Instead it is considered to be a rather extreme variation of the basic *pallidulus*. It should be noted that the name *N. triandrus* var. *albus* is not used at all. The wide range of white, off-white, and cream forms previously sold under this name must now be considered as *N. triandrus* subsp. *triandrus*, a catch-all which I find most unsatisfactory.

We have already mentioned the third subspecies—*N. triandrus* subsp. *capax* from Brittany. The distinction between this bulb and other forms depends upon the length of the corona, which should measure from 9/16 to 1 in. (15–25 mm), but I have flowering at this time a number of bulbs which clearly fall into this category, yet which come from Portugal.

Section 8

Section #8 *Bulbocodii*. *N. bulbocodium* is now listed as the basic species found throughout Spain, Portugal, and south west France, with *N. bulbocodium* subsp. *bulbocodium* as the main subspecies. In this we must now include, as varieties only, the following:

N. bulbocodium var. *citrinus*, *N. bulbocodium* var.*conspicuus*, *N. bulbocodium* var. *filifolius*, *N. bulbocodium* var. *graellsii*, *N. bulbocodium* var. *nivalis*, and *N. bulbocodium* var. *vulgaris*.

A second subspecies in this section is *N. bulbocodium* subsp. *obesus* with its distinct rather fleshy foliage, short stems and wide open, obese coronas of a bright yellow.

The only white-flowered bulbocodium in Europe is *N. cantabricus* and other names previously applied to white-flowered forms are now considered to be varieties of *N. cantabricus*. These include *N. cantabricus* var. *monophyllus* and *N. cantabricus* var. *clusii*.

The quite substantial number of *N. bulbocodium* variants and relatives found in north Africa have not been affected so far by any recent publications, although I understand that a review is under way from Michael Salmon. In the meantime the situation appears to be as follows: *N. cantabricus* is found in north Africa thus providing one of the links between the European and African populations. The well-known *N. petunioides* is considered a variety only of *N. cantabricus*.

N. cantabricus var. *tananicus* is, according to Michael Salmon, incorrectly named, and in saying this he is referring to the bulb, widely distributed and grown under this name, which is a white-flowered *bulbocodium* of moderate size and with a fairly wide-flared corona. It is distinguished mainly by the fact that many flowers are held almost vertically on top of the stem. Michael Salmon suggests that this plant is a form of *N. bulbocodium* subsp. *albidus*, and that the true *N. tananicus* is a more vigorous plant producing taller and quite stiff stems up to 10 in. (25 cm) in height. Large white flowers are produced at right angles on this stem. It flowers in early January.

N. romieuxii is one of the main African forms and many selections have been made. There is serious doubt that the form known as N. mesatlanticus is a really valid subspecies. When viewing both bulbs in bloom it seems clear that mesatlanticus is, in fact, a slight variant of N. romieuxii. Most of the N. romieuxii are pale yellow of varying shades of intensity, but there are white flowered forms which are known as N. romieuxii subsp. albidus. However, here again many bulbs sold with an "albidus" label are pale yellow, and some even have a distinct greenish overtone.

Section 9

Section #9 Pseudonarcissus. Only two bulbs in this section are affected by name changes, and the remainder are not miniatures. First is N. alpestris which is now merged into N. moschatus, although it is less than half the size, and in the dwarf yellow trumpets only N. asturiensis and N. minor are mentioned. This means that such plants as N. nanus and N. pumilus are only considered as variants of N. minor.

This brings us to the end of the proposed changes in names and species rank for all the bulbs normally classed as miniatures. A list of these proposed changes is provided at the end of this chapter.

Computer Data Printouts

Daffodils have now been grown and hybridized for well over 300 years, with particular emphasis in the last century.

As the reader might suppose, the result has been a simply horrendous list of names, many now obsolete, and with numerous duplications. As the flowers produced by the hybridists became more complicated, some with large coronas, others with smaller coronas, and many with multiple bands of colors, the recording of this information became extremely difficult and onerous. In 1977 by general consent, previous methods of classification were revised to include a method of quickly identifying the type of flower, and also to include a color code, so that complete information could be seen and understood at a glance. A reprint of the plan as outlined in the excellent catalog of Rathowen Daffodils of Omagh, Co. Tyrone, Northern Ireland, is presented here with their permission. The use of this system has enabled vital statistics to be assembled on a computer, and printouts can be obtained in many areas, or complete, for thousands of cultivars. The computer database will ultimately cover every Narcissus grown.

PROPOSED NAME CHANGES, based primarily upon Flora Europaea 1980. Not all of these may be accepted in the new Daffodil Register because in many instances they alter the scheme of Fernandes 1968.

N. alpestris = N. moschatus var. alpestris
N. bulbocodium var. citrinus = N. bulbocodium subsp. bulbocodium var. citrinus
N. bulbocodium var. clusii = N. cantabricus var. clusii
N. bulbocodium var. conspicuus = N. bulbocodium subsp. bulbocodium var. conspicuus
N. bulbocodium var. filiformis = N. bulbocodium subsp. bulbocodium var. filiformis
N. bulbocodium var. graellsii = N. bulbocodium subsp. bulbocodium var. graellsii
N. bulbocodium var. monophyllus = N. cantabricus
N. bulbocodium var. nivalis = N. bulbocodium subsp. bulbocodium var. nivalis
N. bulbocodium var. tananicus = N. albidus subsp. tananicus
N. bulbocodium subsp. vulgaris = N. bulbocodium subsp. bulbocodium
N. juncifolius = N. requienii = N. assoanus
N. nanus = N. minor var. nanus

N. pumilus = *N. minor* var. *pumilus*
N. rupicola subsp. *pedunculatus* = *N. cuatrecasasii*
N. triandrus albus = *N. triandrus* subsp. *triandrus*
N. triandrus aurantiacus = *N. triandrus* subsp. *pallidulus* var. *aurantiacus*
N. triandrus cernuus = *N. triandrus* subsp. *pallidulus* var. *cernuus*
N. triandrus concolor = *N. triandrus* subsp. *pallidulus*
N. triandrus subsp. *loiseleuri* = *N. triandrus* subsp. *capax*
N. triandrus pulchellus = *N. triandrus* subsp. *pallidulus* var. *pulchellus*
N. tazetta var. *canaliculatus* = *N. italicus* var. *laticolor*

ADS APPROVED LIST OF MINIATURES

Divisions 1—9 and 12

Agnes Harvey 5 W-W	Hors d'Oeuvre 8 Y-Y	Pencrebar 4 Y-Y
Angie 8 W-W	Hummingbird 6 Y-Y	Pequeneta 7 Y-Y
April Tears 5 Y-Y	Icicle 5 W-W	Petit Buerre 1 Y-Y
Arctic Morn 5 W-W	Jessamy 12 W-W	Picarillo 2 Y-Y
Atom 6 Y-Y	Jetage 6 Y-Y	Piccolo 1 Y-Y
Baby Moon 7 Y-Y	Jumblie 6 Y-O	Picoblanco 3 W-W
Baby Star 7 Y-Y	Junior Miss 6 W-W	Pixie 7 Y-Y
Bagatelle 1 Y-Y	Kehelland 4 Y-Y	Pixie's Sister 7 Y-Y
Bebop 7 W-Y	Kenellis 12 W-Y	Pledge 1 W-W
Bobbysoxer 7 Y-YYO	Kibitzer 6 Y-Y	Poplin 12 Y-Y
Bowle's Bounty 1 Y-Y	Kidling 7 Y-Y	Poppet 5 W-W
Candlepower 1 W-W	Laura 5 W-W	Quince 6 Y-Y
Charles Warren 1 Y-Y	Likely Lad 1 Y-Y	Raindrop 5 W-W
Chit Chat 7 Y-Y	Lilliput 1 W-Y	Rikki 7 W-Y
Clare 7 Y-Y	Little Beauty 1 W-Y	Rockery Beauty 1 W-Y
Cobweb 5 W-Y	Little Gem 1 Y-Y	Rockery Gem 1 W-W
Cricket 7 Y-Y	Little Prince 7 Y-O	Rockery White 1 W-W
Curlylocks 7 Y-Y	Lively Lady 5 W-W	Rosaline Murphy 2 Y-Y
Cyclataz 8 Y-O	Marionette 2 Y-YYR	Rupert 1 W-Y
Demure 7 W-Y	Marychild 12 Y-Y	Sea Gift 7 Y-Y
Doublebois 5 W-W	Mary Plumstead 5 Y-Y	Segovia 3 W-Y
Elfhorn 12 Y-Y	Mini-cycla 6 Y-Y	Sennocke 5 Y-Y
Fairy Chimes 5 Y-Y	Minidaf 1 Y-Y	Shrew 8 W-Y
Flomay 7 W-WPP	Minnow 8 W-Y	Shrimp 5 Y-Y
Flute 6 Y-Y	Mite 6 Y-Y	Sir Echo 1 Y-W
Flyaway 6 Y-Y	Mitzy 6 W-W	Skelmersdale Gold 1 Y-Y
Frosty Morn 5 W-W	Morwenna 2 Y-Y	Skiffle 7 Y-Y
Gambas 1 Y-Y	Muslin 12 W-W	Small Talk 1 Y-Y
Gipsy Queen 1 Y-WWY	Mustard Seed 2 Y-Y	Sneezy 1 Y-Y
Greenshank 6 Y-Y	Nylon 12 W-W	Snipe 6 W-W
Halingy 8 W-Y	Opening Bid 6 Y-Y	Snug 1 W-W
Hawera 5 Y-Y	Pango 8 W-Y	Soltar 6 Y-Y
Heide 6 Y-Y	Paula Cottell 3 W-WWY	Sprite 1 W-W
Hifi 7 Y-Y	Pease-blossom 7 Y-Y	Stafford 7 Y-O

Stella Turk 6 Y-Y
Sun Disc 7 Y-Y
Sundial 7 Y-Y
Taffeta 12 W-W
Tanagra 1 Y-Y
Tarlatan 12 W-W

Tete-a-Tete 6 Y-O
Tiny Tot 1 Y-Y
Tosca 1 W-Y
Tweeny 2 W-Y
W. P. Milner 1 W-W
Wee Bee 1 Y-Y

Wideawake 7 Y-Y
Wren 4 Y-Y
Xit 3 W-W
Yellow Xit 3 W-Y
Zip 6 Y-Y

Division 10

asturiensis Y-Y
atlanticus W-W
bulbocodium (various) Y-Y
°°bulb. tananicus W-W = cantabricus tananicus
calcicola Y-Y
canaliculatus W-Y
cantabricus (various) W-W
cyclamineus Y-Y
dubius W-W
Eystettensis Y-Y (double)
fernandesii Y-Y
gaditanus Y-Y
hedraeanthus Y-Y
jonquilla Y-Y
jonquilla Flora Pleno Y-Y
jonquilla henriquesii Y-Y
jonquilla var. minor Y-Y
jonquilliodes Y-Y
juncifolius Y-Y (now requienii)
°°× macleayii W-Y = × imcomparabilis
minor (various) Y-Y
minor var. pumilus Plenus Y-Y (Rip Van Winkle)
pseudonarcissus subsp. alpestris W-W
pseudonarcissus subsp. bicolor W-Y
rupicola Y-Y
scaberulus Y-Y
tazetta subsp. bertolonii Y-Y
× tenuior W-Y
°°triandrus albus W-W = triandrus var. triandrus
triandrus aurantiacus Y-Y
triandrus cernuus W-W
triandrus concolor Y-Y
triandrus loiseleurii W-W (now capax)
triandrus pulchelus Y-W
watieri W-W
willkommii Y-Y

× = wild hybrid
°° = as listed in 1969 Classified List and International Register of Daffodil Names

Rathowen daffodils

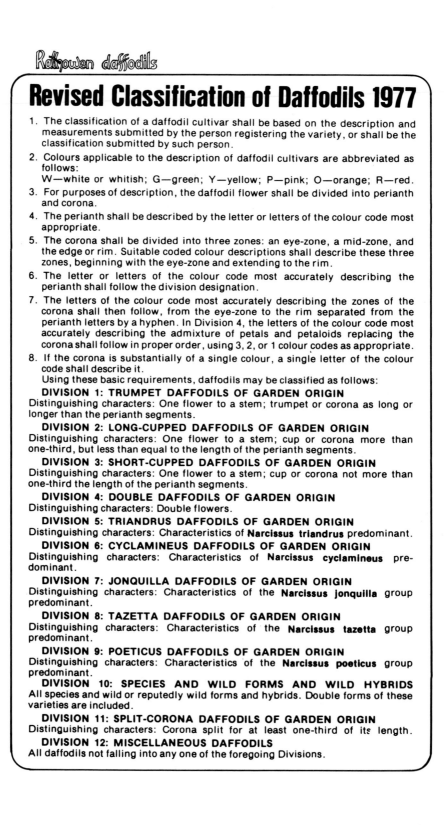

Revised Classification of Daffodils 1977

1. The classification of a daffodil cultivar shall be based on the description and measurements submitted by the person registering the variety, or shall be the classification submitted by such person.

2. Colours applicable to the description of daffodil cultivars are abbreviated as follows:
   W—white or whitish; G—green; Y—yellow; P—pink; O—orange; R—red.

3. For purposes of description, the daffodil flower shall be divided into perianth and corona.

4. The perianth shall be described by the letter or letters of the colour code most appropriate.

5. The corona shall be divided into three zones: an eye-zone, a mid-zone, and the edge or rim. Suitable coded colour descriptions shall describe these three zones, beginning with the eye-zone and extending to the rim.

6. The letter or letters of the colour code most accurately describing the perianth shall follow the division designation.

7. The letters of the colour code most accurately describing the zones of the corona shall then follow, from the eye-zone to the rim separated from the perianth letters by a hyphen. In Division 4, the letters of the colour code most accurately describing the admixture of petals and petaloids replacing the corona shall follow in proper order, using 3, 2, or 1 colour codes as appropriate.

8. If the corona is substantially of a single colour, a single letter of the colour code shall describe it.

   Using these basic requirements, daffodils may be classified as follows:

DIVISION 1: TRUMPET DAFFODILS OF GARDEN ORIGIN
Distinguishing characters: One flower to a stem; trumpet or corona as long or longer than the perianth segments.

DIVISION 2: LONG-CUPPED DAFFODILS OF GARDEN ORIGIN
Distinguishing characters: One flower to a stem; cup or corona more than one-third, but less than equal to the length of the perianth segments.

DIVISION 3: SHORT-CUPPED DAFFODILS OF GARDEN ORIGIN
Distinguishing characters: One flower to a stem; cup or corona not more than one-third the length of the perianth segments.

DIVISION 4: DOUBLE DAFFODILS OF GARDEN ORIGIN
Distinguishing characters: Double flowers.

DIVISION 5: TRIANDRUS DAFFODILS OF GARDEN ORIGIN
Distinguishing characters: Characteristics of **Narcissus triandrus** predominant.

DIVISION 6: CYCLAMINEUS DAFFODILS OF GARDEN ORIGIN
Distinguishing characters: Characteristics of **Narcissus cyclamineus** predominant.

DIVISION 7: JONQUILLA DAFFODILS OF GARDEN ORIGIN
Distinguishing characters: Characteristics of the **Narcissus jonquilla** group predominant.

DIVISION 8: TAZETTA DAFFODILS OF GARDEN ORIGIN
Distinguishing characters: Characteristics of the **Narcissus tazetta** group predominant.

DIVISION 9: POETICUS DAFFODILS OF GARDEN ORIGIN
Distinguishing characters: Characteristics of the **Narcissus poeticus** group predominant.

DIVISION 10: SPECIES AND WILD FORMS AND WILD HYBRIDS
All species and wild or reputedly wild forms and hybrids. Double forms of these varieties are included.

DIVISION 11: SPLIT-CORONA DAFFODILS OF GARDEN ORIGIN
Distinguishing characters: Corona split for at least one-third of its length.

DIVISION 12: MISCELLANEOUS DAFFODILS
All daffodils not falling into any one of the foregoing Divisions.

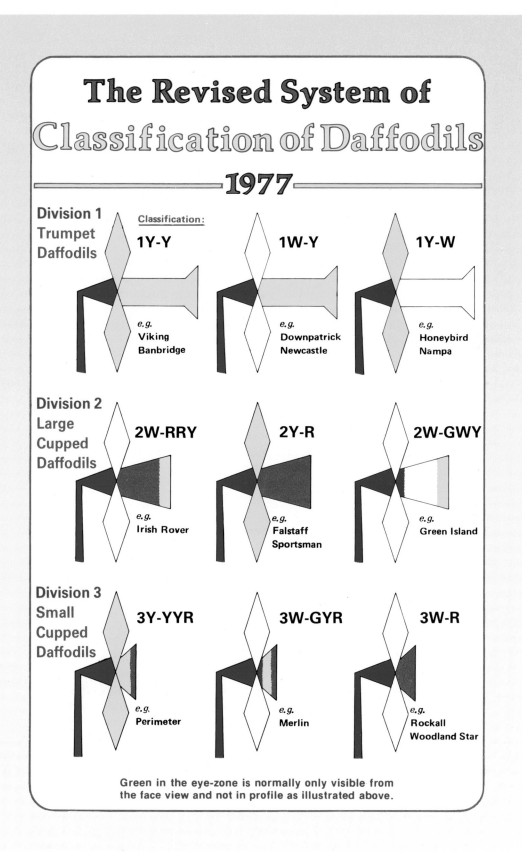

The Revised System of
Classification of Daffodils
1977

**Division 1
Trumpet
Daffodils**

Classification:

1Y-Y

e.g.
Viking
Banbridge

1W-Y

e.g.
Downpatrick
Newcastle

1Y-W

e.g.
Honeybird
Nampa

**Division 2
Large
Cupped
Daffodils**

2W-RRY

e.g.
Irish Rover

2Y-R

e.g.
Falstaff
Sportsman

2W-GWY

e.g.
Green Island

**Division 3
Small
Cupped
Daffodils**

3Y-YYR

e.g.
Perimeter

3W-GYR

e.g.
Merlin

3W-R

e.g.
Rockall
Woodland Star

**Green in the eye-zone is normally only visible from
the face view and not in profile as illustrated above.**

CHAPTER TWO

Outdoor Cultivation

For most enthusiasts the acquisition and growing of miniature daffodils is aimed at showing the flowers in regional or national flower shows in the competitive classes open only to these types. For this purpose, growing outside is almost essential, although the rules of exhibiting do permit most miniatures to be grown in a 'protected area' such as a frame, whereas standard cultivars must be grown in the open. Outdoor cultivation is therefore considered first as being the method of widest general interest. But I find it necessary to note that, in my opinion, outdoor cultivation is quite unsatisfactory for many of the really charming and desirable species, which because of size, constitution, or the character of their native environment, just do not lend themselves to the rough and tumble of the average winter, whether in North America or elsewhere. There is, in my judgement, a considerable list of species, as well as a number of the truly *miniature* hybrids which require pan culture in a cool frame or greenhouse. The required microclimates can be provided in such structures so the bulbs are protected from the ravages of winter, predators, and similar hazards not usual to their native heath. Then, and only then, can the full beauty of these plants be seen and appreciated. But there are many hybrids and just a few species to which these limitations do not apply. How should we deal with these?

Daffodils are not fussy as to soil. Any good, well-worked garden soil will grow them well, nor are they exacting as to whether the soil is acid or alkaline.

The one requirement which is absolutely essential is good drainage. Although descriptions of some of the wild species note that they were found growing on the banks of streams, in boggy areas, and at times even under running water, these reports should not be construed to suggest that bulbs will grow best under similar conditions, even if your garden can provide them. Good drainage is the first essential, and if natural drainage of either the site or the top soil is in doubt, it must be modified until it is, without question, well drained. Can we define this? Yes, to some extent. Dig a hole where you propose to plant your bulbs about as wide and as deep as a normal 5 gallon (20 l) bucket. Then fill the hole with water—about 5 gallons. It should drain away completely within 10 minutes after being poured into the hole. If it takes longer, then perhaps the soil and certainly the sub-soil requires opening to allow the water to drain more readily.

If you are unfortunately dealing with a naturally heavy, sticky soil, the work necessary to change the soil mixture may be more substantial. The one obvious method is to prepare an area as a raised bed, 9–12 in. (22–30 cm) above the general level, and fill the bed with prepared compost. This is costly and demanding but if the basic soil is really difficult this may well be the easiest way out. Naturally heavy soil can be greatly improved by the application of heavy dressings of gypsum at rates up to 8 oz. per square yard. (260 g per sq. m) Gypsum induces the particles of clay in the soil to group together, or flocculate, thus providing spaces which allow water to drain through more readily. However the process is slow and results are not always certain. Mixing in any coarse, rough, humus material such as well rotted compost, plus grit and even small stones will help; but substantial quantities will be required which should be mixed into the soil to a good depth by double digging. This is again a laborious task.

In most cases however, the typical gardener is dealing with a fairly easily worked, friable top soil. In such cases, good deep digging plus the incorporation of a fair amount of well rotted compost, or peat if compost is not available, will suffice.

Ideally the bed should be worked over by digging and adding either compost or peat from a previous crop, i.e. a year in advance of planting bulbs. Clearing this first crop, whatever it may be, and the digging of the bed to prepare for planting, thoroughly mixes any additives, so that the soil condition is even and uniform. On one small point all growers agree: Do NOT use any fresh manure, even if available, or any form of fertilizer which is high in nitrogen. High nitrogen levels stimulate tall, lush growth of leaves, and soft, unthrifty bulbs which are much more likely to be affected by basal rot. On normal, well worked soils, a good dressing with wood ashes, or of sulphate of potash, is all that is needed.

Although it hardly applies to bulbs, there is an old nurseryman's saying that for a $1.00 plant you should dig a $10.00 hole. What this means is that under average conditions you can hardly overdo the basic preparations, *unless you become heavy handed with artificial additives.* Normal cultivations which include the addition and thorough mixing of organic materials such as peat, leaf mould or well-rotted compost can hardly be overdone.

'Marionette'. A good miniature for the open border.

Next comes the matter of sterilization. Can and should this be carried out on an outdoor area in which bulbs are to be planted? Yes it can: and if your aim is to ensure really excellent results, as well as to avoid much of the drugery of weeding and the hazards of disease, some form of sterilization is recommended.

When talking of sterilization most gardeners have visions of a complicated process, costly and difficult to perform. This is no longer true, for chemical methods of soil sterilization are now available which are comparatively easy to use, and completely effective if done properly.

There are a number of materials available, both liquid and granular. All essentially have to release a gas into the soil which kills every living organism before it is dissipated into the air. Methylbromide is one which is most effective, but awkward to use, while the material with which I am most familiar is a liquid called Vapam®. This is not a very pleasant material to handle, although it is not dangerous. Considerable care must be taken in handling the liquid and applying it, because the fumes are unpleasant, and the liquid highly corrosive. It must therefore be handled with care, using rubber gloves and a protective apron. Should a small amount of the concentrate splash onto the skin it must be washed off immediately. This sounds as if it is deadly, which it is not, but it can be most unpleasant if not handled with care.

Soil to be sterilized must be open, slightly moist, well worked and at a temperature of 60°F (15°C) or above. Vapam® is applied to the surface of the soil at the rate of 1 pint (0.5 l) per 100 sq. ft. (30 sq. m). To apply this amount evenly and effectively use a simple proportionator, such as a Hozon®, so that the liquid to be applied can be bulked up to allow for even distribution.

Vapam® can be diluted with water to almost any degree, so water is used as a carrier to spread the Vapam® evenly across the area to be treated. Once the required amount has been applied, the soil should be saturated with water to carry the Vapam® down to the depth to which the soil is to be sterilized. If the desired level is at least 12 in. (30 cm) then the small amount of Vapam® spread upon the surface must be driven down to this level by applying substantial amounts of water through a sprinkler or hose. The extra water will seal the surface, thus retaining the Vapam® within the soil until the job is done. The liquid Vapam® eventually turns into a gas which is what actually sterilizes the soil. The escape of this gas is slowed down by the water seal, but the whole system can be made even more efficient if the area is covered with a sheet of plastic after the Vapam® has been applied and watered in. Leave the bed covered for at least four days, then remove the plastic and cultivate the top layer so that the water seal is broken. If the weather is warm and fine, a week may be required for all the gas to escape. It should be remembered that any fall of natural water—rain—which comes after the plastic is removed will delay the escape of the gas, so more time is needed to be sure it is clear.

How can one be sure that the soil is fit to plant? Quite simply. First dig down into the soil and smell the moist earth below. If the slightest hint of Vapam® can be noticed, it has not all gone. But an infallible test is to attempt to germinate lettuce seed in treated soil. Take any large jar with a tight screw top and half fill with moist soil taken from below the surface, and in which a faint odor of Vapam® remains. Place a moist pad of paper towelling on top of the soil and place on this pad a few lettuce seeds previously moistened. Screw the top of the jar on tightly and place on a well lighted window sill. If there is even one part per million of Vapam® left in the soil, the lettuce seed will not germinate. But if it is clear, the seed will begin to sprout in 48 hours. If roots can be seen coming from the seeds the soil is fit to plant.

But why all this fuss? What will Vapam® do? Vapam® is the nearest thing there is to steam sterilization. Properly applied, Vapam® will kill every weed seed and every disease organism that may be in the soil: nematodes, fungi, insects, everything. The soil is rendered free of all harmful organisms and as with other forms of sterilization, seems to give a great boost to the beneficial organisms, and thus produces quite astonishing growth in the subsequent crop. Remember, however, that Vapam® will kill all plants, so the ground must be absolutely clear, and great care taken to see that the chemical is not inadvertently spread to adjacent areas where valuable plants may be growing.

How to Plant

To my mind, no matter how daffodils are grown, they are most effective in a clump or group, rather than as individuals. This is even more true of the miniatures, for by reason of their limited stature and relative dainty blooms, the best effect can only be obtained from a group of at least five bulbs, more if possible. Such groups will multiply in ensuing years until there is a well established clump, producing a number of flowers. Most miniature bulbs are quite small, some extremely so, and the depth of planting must be governed, at least in part, by the type of bulb and its eventual habit of growth. If grown outside, most bulbs, even the smallest, should have at least 2 in. (5 cm) of soil above them to provide some degree of winter protection. This point is of considerable importance in many areas in North America where winters can be both extreme and of long duration. In these more northerly climes, additional protection may be needed in the form of a good mulch, applied in the fall—November, December—which is removed in the spring once the soil has thawed. In more reasonable areas, where prolonged and severe freezing is not typical, mulching is not necessary.

When to Plant

The ideal time is in August if the bulbs are to hand. However, bulbs are rarely available for sale at this time, most coming into the stores in late September. So planting should be undertaken as soon as the bulbs can be obtained. The whole of the month of September is fine as is the month of October, but any later may not yield such good results. Daffodils commence to root after their resting period is over in the summer. As temperatures drop and the soil is moistened by autumn rains, new roots are produced from the root plate and the bulb prepares for the normal spring surge of growth. Lower temperatures and perhaps freezing of the soil brings this rooting process to a halt during the depth of winter, but as temperatures rise in the spring growth recommences. Under normal conditions, the tips of the new leaves can be seen quite early in the spring—sometimes too early! There is no doubt that if new bulbs can be planted before the end of October results are better, but if the bulbs are received later for some reason, do not despair, for although the results in the first season may not be satisfactory, bulbs quickly adjust so the next year results will be fine.

Basal Rot

Although this fungus problem will be dealt with at greater length in the chapter dealing with pests and diseases, it is appropriate to consider it here, for it is an ever present problem. If present in the soil, the disease attacks any Narcissus bulb, entering through the scars produced by the new roots as they emerge from the root plate, then spreading through the bulb and eventually killing it. The problem can be minimized first by sterilization of the soil with Vapam®, and secondly by treating each bulb with a protective fungicide powder before planting. It must also be recognized that some Narcissus, both species and cultivars, are highly susceptible to the disease while others are equally resistant. But it has been clearly proven that all bulbs are greatly aided by having a soak treatment with Benlate before planting. The solution is made by mixing 2 level tablespoons of 50% Benlate in one gallon of water, (2 gms/1) mixing the Benlate in a small amount of hot water first to ensure that it is completely dissolved. If bulbs are being lifted for storing, after cleaning and drying, they should be dipped in the Benlate solution for at least 30 minutes before hanging up the net bag to dry for storing. The same soak treatment should be repeated before the bulbs are planted, but it is not necessary to dry the bulbs again before planting; they can be planted wet. If this Benlate soak is difficult, then I have developed what I call a shotgun mixture of fungicides, mixed together as powders, in which the root plate of bulbs is dipped just before planting. This may not be quite so effective for some bulbs but it serves for most. I have used this powder for some years now on all my Narcissus and have reduced problems with basal rot to the point where I give little thought to it, except with those species and hybrids known to be prone to the disease (see Chapter Five).

Subsequent Care

If the preparation of the growing area is thorough, the bulbs healthy when planted, and the bases dipped in the fungicide mix, then they should establish quickly and grow without difficulty. Some measure of protection to the top of the bed may be desirable where conditions are severe, but a mulch, if used, should not be too deep, and should be largely removed early in the spring. Label each group carefully and make a clear record or map of the bed on paper so if a label is lost or removed, each group can be pinpointed. Keep the bed free from weeds and enjoy it.

Once flowering is completed the dead flowers should be removed and as the foliage begins to die down it should also be removed. The surface of the bed should be regularly cultivated. A loose friable soil will go a long way to discourage both the larger narcissus fly, *Merodon equestris* as well as the lesser narcissus bulb fly, *Eumerus tuberculatus,* for both are just as partial to the bulbs of most miniature cultivars as the standard types (see Chapter Five).

Plantings will remain vigorous for at least two growing seasons, and more often three. By the end of the third season some bulbs will clearly be in excellent condition, with no decrease in the number of flowers produced. These can be left undisturbed, but others, mainly by producing fewer flowers and more foliage, indicate a heavy splitting of the bulbs into small offsets, none of which have the room to develop into a good flowering size bulb. These bulbs need lifting and replanting. Lifting can be done at any time eight weeks after flowering even if the bulbs still maintain green foliage. In the eight weeks following flowering the bulbs will have grown and established embryo flowers for the following year. Bulbs then can be lifted at any time, say, after the end of June, with no adverse effect upon their subsequent flowering. The bulbs should be lifted carefully, group by group, and be allowed to dry for a few hours only on the surface of the bed. They should then be cleaned by removing dead and dying leaves and soil, gathered into plastic net bags together with label, and immediately given a Benlate dip. Once this is complete the bags can be hung up to dry, and then stored until planting time, keeping them as cool as possible.

The bulbs should be examined again before planting for any sign of disease. Discard anything that looks doubtful, and in particular any bulbs which appear soft, for these are quite likely to contain a grub of the bulb fly.

If the bulbs are doing well, increase by natural division can be considerable. The rate of increase varies from species to species, but most of the cultivars and many of the species can increase with quite alarming speed. One is forced to find either new areas to plant or start an active exchange program with other growers.

A complete list of both species and miniature cultivars suitable for outdoor culture is given in Appendix C.

'Sundial'. One of Alec Gray's jonquil hybrids, excellent for the garden.

CHAPTER THREE

Indoor Cultivation in a Frame or Cool Greenhouse

If there is one group of bulbs which is exactly suited for indoor cultivation, it is miniature daffodils. Not only can they be grown with great success in this way, but many of the more delicate, small species, as well as the most diminutive cultivars, demand controlled conditions if they are to be grown to perfection. As Alec Gray puts it in his book *Miniature Daffodils*, "To enjoy the beauty of individual blooms such as those of *N. watieri* they must be grown in pans so that they can be seen more or less at eye level: only the very young really enjoy crawling about on the ground." I could not agree with him more.

But there are other compelling reasons. For many of the diminutive species a fair measure of control of the micro-climate both above and below ground is essential to success. Consider if you will that the natural home of many of these species is an exposed hilltop or mountain in Spain, Portugal or Morocco. They have adapted very exactly to the natural conditions found in these places and do not take kindly to high temperatures with excessive rain in mid-summer, when they are adapted to being completely dry and sunbaked. Still others require a fair amount of water when growing, but nothing much after flowering is complete. Others are not used to violent fluctuations in winter temperatures, such as deep freezes in December with a week long thaw in February, followed by more freezing weather. These conditions which are part and parcel of the typical North American climate are not normal for Spain, and certainly not at all for Morocco. Why then should we expect bulbs adapted to different conditions to become acclimatized at once to our conditions, whatever they may be? It is unreasonable to expect this and yet the litany of lament and failure continues from people who aspire to see and enjoy *N. romieuxii*, yet are strongly opposed to providing these bulbs with something more closely approximating their native habitat.

The final point in favor of growing bulbs indoors is that many of the species and some of the early hybrids, particularly in the Bulbocodium group, commence to flower well before Christmas, and if they are growing outside, disaster is built in. Species with such a precocious habit must have some protection, as must most of the cultivars resulting from crosses of the early flowering forms.

A well planned collection of pans containing species and miniature cultivars from most of the main *Narcissus* divisions can commence blooming in mid-October, pass through a substantial display starting in late November, through December, January, February and into early March, finally fading slowly with a few latecomers in late March and early April. As the last flowers fade in the pans the normal season for most of the sturdier species and miniature cultivars is just beginning in the garden. One can therefore look forward to a second display through

April and into May, with a few remaining blooms late in that month. It is thus quite feasible to have some form of narcissus in bloom for at least eight months, with the added interest of seeing in comfort and close quarters blooms which are produced to perfection only under cool greenhouse conditions.

When I first became interested in these bulbs, I was fortunate to meet and talk to John Blanchard, an amateur grower and breeder of daffodils in England. He has most ably and efficiently taken on the mantle of growing and hybridizing minia-ture daffodils previously worn by Alec Gray. John Blanchard also grows and hybridizes standard types, for which he has received many awards. But that is another story. Suffice it to say that he is an acknowledged expert, following in his father's footsteps and developing still further the many interesting hybrids which originated in Blandford. John Blanchard grows practically all his miniature bulbs, both species and cultivars, in pans in a cool greenhouse, i.e. a glass house without any means of heating. In England, where the normal winter is not too severe, closing the house tightly is usually sufficient protection. If the house freezes then the bulbs are brought to a standstill and as a result many of his species and hybrids bloom in his house well after Christmas, or nearer to their usual time were they grown outside. Both John and his father experimented with miniature species and cultivars in the open garden, and found that some prefer an open ground culture while others did not.

A case in point is the well known hybrid 'April Tears,' one of Alec Gray's best. This did not grow or flower well for the Blanchards when maintained in pans, but once planted out it developed strongly and flowered profusely. Clearly there is no absolute rule of thumb. The individual needs of each species or cultivar must be understood, and where possible, met. However there still remains a substantial group which do prosper under gentle and controlled conditions, and it is to these that we now address ourselves.

The methods which I use have been developed over a period of years, starting as a close adaptation of John Blanchard's methods, adjusting them slightly to meet my own and local North American conditions. My house is a standard-type green-house with a rather high peak roof to carry a heavy snow load if necessary. In other areas the peak could well be lower. It is attached to my home so that I can walk out of our dining room through a wide door directly into the greenhouse. It measures 14 ft. (4.3 m) wide by 25 ft. (7.5 m) long and is covered to the ground with fiber glass, which replaced the original glass after a devastating ice storm. This material must be carefully cleaned once a year with strong Clorox (the standard household chlorine bleach) diluted with some water. Wiping down the fiber glass particularly outside, removes all dust and algae which accumulates. It greatly increases light penetration for the coming year. This cleaning is done annually before planting the bulbs in August. Four foot (1.2 M) wide benches run down both sides of the house. These are built rather low, not more than 2½ ft. (0.8 m) above the floor so that it is easy to stretch across the full width of the bench from the center aisle. The center space is quite wide, and is used to accommodate larger plants in tubs for over-wintering, and at times to store pans which have finished blooming on the benches. Each bench is constructed of angle iron welded in place, the base made of currugated asbestos sheets which lie inside resting on the angle iron. The currugea-tions are filled with grit to level the base of the bench and to ensure good drainage. The benches are edged with 6 in. (15 cm) high boards of treated wood. The bench is finally filled with at least 5 in. (12.7 cm) of a 50-50 mixture of peat and perlite used as a plunging medium.

Heat is provided by a small gas heater fixed under the bench at the farthest end from the house. It is thermostatically controlled to provide heat when the temperature drops 40°F (5°C). Ventilation is provided by a small 20 in. (50 cm) fan in the apex of the roof at the far end. It also is thermostatically controlled to commence ventilating at a slow speed when the air temperature reaches 65°F (20°C). If the temperature continues to rise the fan automatically moves to a higher speed.

All my miniature daffodils are grown in earthenware pans or pots. I tried plastic, but because I had difficulty in judging the amount of water required, I reverted to clay. If only plastic is available I am sure they can be managed correctly. It is when you have a mixture of clay and plastic that problems arise.

Once filled, these pans are then plunged into the peat-perlite mix as I find that plunging greatly reduces the speed of water loss. Everything tends to be much more even no matter what the size of pot or pan. The only difference arises when a large pan is full of bulbs with heavy top growth. To keep such a pan even with others less heavily populated requires a little judgment when watering.

I mentioned the cleaning of the fiber glass with Clorox but cleaning should not be confined to the cover. The entire house—benches, floor, walls—must be washed down in August to establish a "kitchen cleanliness" environment. I consider cleanliness to be absolutely essential for success. Any sloppiness in the cleaning, and problems will arise at once.

For this reason all pans are cleaned each year by soaking them in a fairly strong Clorox solution for a few days and then scrubbing them clean. All algae, encrustations of salts, etc. must be removed from both the inside and outside of the pans. I used to leave my bulbs down for two years when I began, and many growers continue to do so successfully. I have found, however, that under my conditions it pays to lift and check the bulbs in every pan each summer. I can then judge as to how they have grown, eliminate any doubtful or diseased specimens, and plant back a selected group of sound, clean bulbs which I feel sure will do well the following spring. It also gives me the opportunity to remove certain bulbs which were marked while in growth as perhaps not being true to name, or which have a peculiar characteristic I would like to examine more closely and separately. Rogues can be removed and the stock maintained even and clean. Any surplus can also be determined and used for sale or exchange.

If the pans are shaken out and the bulbs sorted and cleaned in late June or early July, replanting can be undertaken at any convenient time from the middle of August onwards. Some of the bulbocodiums really prefer not to be out of the ground at all, for they hardly ever enter complete dormancy. *N. bulbocodium* var. *graellsii*, for example, usually blooms in late April or early May. By the end of June the bulbs are still in active growth, and I believe it is best to repot this variant almost at once. *N. cyclamineus* is another which does not seem to require or appreciate a really dry resting period in the summer, for the bulbs tend to dry up and shrivel out of the ground. Although they seem to recover, as when they are received from a commercial supplier, I cannot think that the condition is ideal. So I usually move *N. cyclamineus* quite quickly into its new pan. But all the others, especially the forms of *N. bulbocodium* and *N. jonquilla*, which may have originated in southern Spain or Morocco seem to require a period of real baking under hot dry conditions.

This then is another reason for having bulbs under control, in pans and in a greenhouse. When I first began growing and the season's bloom was over I reasoned that the bulbs would come to natural maturity much better if they were placed outside on a bed of gravel and allowed to die down. My whole stock was removed outside at the end of April and the move happened to coincide with the onset of a period of heavy rain. With no experience to go by, I began to be apprehensive after a week, and with the help of my wife all pans were brought back inside once more. Later when the bulbs were cleaned, I discovered just how important it is to avoid such conditions. Losses were substantial among certain species, particularly among all forms of *triandrus*. This convinced me that for miniature daffodils as a group some degree of control is desirable, a position I have maintained ever since.

Some cultivars which have appeared to be somewhat too large for pan culture, or of sufficiently robust habit as to warrant open air growing, have been moved outside. As a result I now have two collections which inevitably overlap, one predominantly in pans and the other in a prepared border in the garden.

Soil Mixes

There are numerous growing media available, so the grower may well be confused when faced with a mountain of plastic bags offering every conceivable type. What should one use?

Here is what I do. I operate fairly closely to one of the English formulas known as the J. I. (John Innes) mixes. The basic mix calls for

7 parts by volume of loam (not too light, not too heavy)
3 parts by volume of peat
2 parts by volume of coarse grit (sold as traction grit by most hardware stores)

This mix then requires the addition of a base fertilizer available in England but not North America. I have compromised by using as the source of peat a material sold as Pro Mix which is a peat, perlite, vermiculite mix containing a modest amount of base fertilizer. Pro Mix is used in place of the three parts of peat. The soil used is good, well-worked garden soil which has never grown daffodils and which has been sterilized using Vapam. (See Chapter 2) Sterilization of soil in a heap is quite simple. The soil is placed on a sheet of strong plastic in layers each about 6 in. (15 cm) deep. To each layer a sprinkling of Vapam mixed with water is applied and then another layer of soil added. Once a good heap has been built, cover it with plastic and allow the internal sun heat to build up for at least a week. Then open and air the soil before finally mixing with the Pro Mix peat and grit.

This then is my basic mix which I modify as occasion demands, by the addition of either more grit or more peat. It is used unaltered for most daffodils which do not have specific requirements. But for some, such as *N. cyclamineus*, more peat is added, and for all the *N. triandrus* forms the quantity of grit may be doubled.

In the 1986–7 Daffodil Yearbook of the R.H.S. an article appeared suggesting the value of completely artificial mixes for growing bulbs in pots or pans.

The following year I tested this idea, using two mixes, applying them to a wide variety of bulbs. All did well and grew without disease problems. One difference was noted, in that there was less natural increase of bulbs in both size and number. With this encouraging result, I have now tried one mix for all my bulbs, and it appears to be doing very well indeed. The mix is made from 75% Pro-Mix and 25% coarse grit. No further adjustments are made for any of the different bulbs. Both *N. cyclamineus* and *N. triandrus* are doing very well, but those known to be difficult, such as *N. triandrus* forms and *N. scaberulus,* are accorded the special treatment as described in Chapter 5. Careful additional feeding is also being applied for a brief period after the bulbs have flowered to aid in the correct development of the bulbs as they move to maturity. I have high hopes that the use of this mix may become standard, removing the multitude of variables associated with soil based mixes.

The pans or pots may vary in size, depending upon the number of bulbs to be planted in any one type or cultivar. If purchasing bulbs from a supplier, perhaps only one can be afforded or if not too expensive, three or even five. For small quantities like this, smaller containers are used, so I usually have a "smorgasbord" of types and sizes available from which to choose.

All pans are crocked with pieces of broken pots, which have also been sterilized in a strong Clorox solution, as disease can easily be brought into the new pots on dirty crocks. I have tried covering the drainage holes with stones, gravel, stone chips, and similar materials, but for some reason which I cannot explain pieces of old pots (crocks) seem best. I now use nothing else and if I am short of crocks I break up a few pots!

With crocks in place, the pan or pot is filled at least half way with compost, the depth below the bulbs depending upon the type and size of the bulbs to be planted. Each bulb is then lightly dipped into my shotgun fungicide mix, so that the base root plate of each bulb is covered. Bulbs are placed quite close, actual spacing depending upon the size and type. I try to fill a pan with bulbs all more or less the same size, leaving second-size bulbs for a second pan. The former should produce a good display of bloom, while the latter produces little or none. However, the bulbs will grow to flowering size for the next season. Bulbs are placed almost touching each other which may result in upwards of 25 small bulbs of one of the dwarf bulbocodiums in a 6 in. (15 cm) pan, but perhaps only 10–12 of say *N. minor* where the bulbs are substantially larger. But quite a number can usually be placed in any pan, for it should be remembered that under this system, the bulbs will be lifted and replanted for the next season. If the bulbs are to be down for two growing seasons, then more space must be left between the bulbs when planting to allow for growth and development during two growing seasons.

When the bulbs are in place, they are covered with more compost until the tops of the bulbs are at least ½ in. (2.5 cm) below the surface. The compost should then be gently firmed and a little more added if necessary to bring the soil level up to within ¼ in. (1.2 cm) of the rim. This surface is then immediately covered with a thin layer of ⅜ in. (2 cm) granite chips. I use a grade that is packaged into 50 lb. (25 kg) bags for landscaping. This layer reduces surface drying and protects it from smearing when being watered. Water falls between the stones and filters quickly into the soil beneath. Each pot is then clearly labelled and plunged into the bench in the peat-perlite mix.

It is important to label while planting, but remember that old labels should not be kept and simply restuck into the new pan, as the base of the label can carry disease. If using semi-permanent labels for reuse, sterilize them before introducing them into the new pan. I always label and number my pans immediately as I work, recording name, number, and pot number onto individual sheets in a small three ring notebook, one species, cultivar or number to a page. I later record all that happens to that pan during the growing season—any peculiarities, any strange bulbs marked to be removed and indeed anything at all of interest on the one sheet. I now have a series of these books in which I can trace each group of bulbs from the day I acquired it to date. I know whether a particular source is good or otherwise and I can compare and contrast on these sheets different lots of ostensibly the same species or cultivar. It is quite usual to purchase three lots of, say *N. bulbocodium* var. *nivalis* and receive three quite different bulbs. These sheets and yearbooks provide a base of recorded experience upon which I can, with luck, make reasonable judgments and selections to establish what I believe to be both the best form, and the most true to name in any species.

With the bulbs planted, plunged and labelled, I may wait some weeks before I give the initial watering. If the compost is quite dry the bulbs will remain dormant

Authors greenhouse. Planting complete.

until such time as they are watered, which may be deferred until sometime in early September. If the plunging material and the compost are quite dry I usually give the initial watering from the hose to gently dampen down the pots and plunging medium. If both media are extremely dry two or three gentle waterings may be needed to bring the entire bench to a uniform moistness. Once this uniform state has been reached I apply a general watering with Benlate, using 2 level tablespoons per gallon (approximately 2 gm per 1), carefully sprinkling everything—pots, bench, plunging medium and surrounding woodwork. This soak down is simply a preventative against fungus problems and an extension of the "kitchen cleanliness" principle.

The house is kept fully ventilated at all times and is not heated until the outside temperature drops close to freezing which is usually not until late November or early December. Then an occasional burst of modest heating may be required to maintain a night temperature of 40°F. (5°C)

First flowers will be seen possibly in late September but certainly in October. Typical fall flowering types will come first, such as *N. serotinus* and *N. humilis*, but before long the first of the white bulbocodiums will be budding. *N. cantabricus* var. *foliosus* followed quickly by *N. cantabricus* subsp. *monophyllus* and others. Usually by Christmas quite a number will be flowering or showing buds, and by mid-January there should be a fine display with many of the jonquils in bloom or coming and the trumpet or pseudonarcissus group well advanced. Flowering will continue through February and March, with a few coming in early April.

Once flowering is well under way, I depart from the norm by applying one or sometimes two light applications of a complete balanced liquid fertilizer. I use a 20-20-20 concentrate, which means that there are equal parts of nitrogen, phosphorus and potash in the mix. One pound (.45 kg) is placed in a full 5 gallon (20 l) bucket of water and dissolved. I apply the fertilizer with a small venturi proportionator called a Hozon (or Siphonex) attached to the water tap. The hose is then attached to the Hozon and the small tube from the Hozon dropped into the bucket of concentrate. When the water is turned on, as it passes through the hose it causes a slight suction which draws the concentrate up through the small tube and mixes it with the out-going water at a ratio of 16 to 1, i.e. for every 16 gallons of water coming through the hose, 1 gallon of concentrate will also be sucked up and mixed with water as it moves out. I find that once the bulbs are in full growth and are beginning to flower a normal watering applied in this way together with a very small amount of balanced fertilizer seems to help the bulb continue growing strongly after flowering. This in turn seems to produce good bulbs which are more likely to flower again the next year. If growth seems slow, or the color of the foliage rather pale, a second dose of fertilizer may be applied in the same way a month or six weeks later, but only if it appears to be necessary. Last year, for instance, I obtained my top soil from a new area in the garden where the soil was apparently much better. As a result all the bulbs grew strongly in the pans so I gave no fertilizer at all. Judgment is needed and if in doubt, do not feed.

As the bulbs finish flowering the dead flowers are removed, keeping only those used for hybridizing, and the water is slowly decreased. It is essential that as the bulbs go into the gentle downgrade after flowering they remain moderately moist but never wet. A wet soil at this time can spell disaster and the loss of many interesting and valuable bulbs. When the leaves clearly begin to turn yellow, water should be withheld and the pots and pans allowed to slowly dry out, together with the surrounding plunging mix. Once completely dry and dormant the bulbs can, with advantage, be cleaned up to remove dead foliage but otherwise be left undisturbed for a month or two, before being shaken out, examined and prepared for replanting.

One or two additional points: All new bulbs received are given a Benlate 30

Narcissus bulbocodium var. *tenuifolius* showing increase by one bulb in one season.

minute soak before planting to ensure that they are as clean as possible. Even so, some bulbs of new stocks will inevitably die, usually from basal rot, or something that looks remarkably like it. If a bulb begins to grow, putting out leaves and then suddenly stops, with the tips of the leaves turning yellow, you can assume that the bulb is diseased. Each season as growth commences I go over all pots and pans with great care, looking for trouble. Using the broad blade of a pocket knife any doubtful bulbs are carefully eased out of the pan and destroyed. The area from which the bulb came is then soaked with Subdue (see Chapter 5) which usually confines the trouble to the one bulb. Occasionally two or even three adjacent bulbs may be affected so these should, in turn be removed.

A second problem may be the obvious development of the virus known as 'stripe' in new leaves as they begin to grow. Certain suppliers seem to be prone to growing bulbs with this disease, probably from the want of care in keeping their stocks clean. The only answer here is ruthlessly to remove all bulbs which show the telltale stripes and burn them. I have found on occasion that while an appearance of stripe may arise in bulbs growing under glass, these same bulbs seem to lose the obvious signs of trouble when grown in the open. However, this is probably due to the deeper green color in the leaves which may tend to hide the yellow stripes. The cause of stripe is a virus which is spread by aphids, and because of this many of the jonquil group have become infected. These bulbs tend to continue growing rather late in the season, some retaining their green foliage into late spring and early summer. Plenty of aphids are abroad by this time and as a result the bulbs can become infected. Rogueing can be hard to do, especially if one has only two or three bulbs, but stocks will never be really clean and virus-free unless this policy is adopted. It is also essential to keep the bulbs free from aphids whether indoors or out. In the greenhouse a regular fumigation with Nicofume will keep them clean, and outdoors a regular spray, also with a nicotine preparation, will do the same.

One final point in connection with pan culture; if you are interested in hybridizing nothing is simpler and easier than the crossing of two flowers in pans. The flowers are clean and undamaged. The pans are elevated, so it is very easy to take anthers from one flower and apply the pollen to another. The development of the seed pods can be watched and the seed gathered as it ripens without difficulty or loss. There is no doubt that the growing of daffodils under cover in pans is most conducive to hybridizing, so much so that one can get carried away and end up with so much seed that one hardly knows what to do with it. Indoor culture also enables the grower to gather pollen from early flowering types, and store it in gelatin capsules in the refrigerator, to use on later blooming species and cultivars. Crosses which would be almost impossible under outdoor conditions become quite simple.

To sum up the methods I have described.
1. *Clean* everything possible to a state of kitchen cleanliness and maintain this standard in every possible way.
2. *Standardize* soil mixes and sterilize the soil so that you know what you have and how the bulbs will behave.
3. *Control* all aspects of growth, flowering, and subsequent development up to the dying down, and keeping the pans under cover at all times.
4. *Ruthlessly* remove all bulbs which appear unhealthy while in growth.
5. *See that all species,* excepting only one or two, receive a real baking during the summer following flowering. This may make the difference between little or no flowering and heavy blooming on many of the species and their first generation hybrids.

CHAPTER FOUR

Hybridizing

With even a modest collection of bulbs in your hands, and with the obvious advantages of clean pans of flowers produced under the controlled conditions in a frame or greenhouse, it is most natural to wonder what might result if this bulb was "married" to that. Might another wonder bulb like 'Tete-a-Tete' be produced? Well you might and under any circumstance hybridizing is a good deal of fun and quite easy to do. Too easy in fact! At this writing I have batches of seed from the last six years, the first lot about to bloom for the second time. As a result I have become aware of a number of pitfalls into which I, together with many others, have already fallen. The problem is that it is so easy to make a cross and to produce a fine fat pod of seed that one tends to go mad, dabbing pollen here and there until one has many pods, each with perhaps from 5 to 100 seeds. At first this may not appear to be a bad thing, but then you must sow them and if you get good germination, you then have pots filled with hundreds of seedlings. What do you do with them? You really want to grow each and every one, for the one you discard might be just the bulb you are seeking. So it quickly becomes a most difficult matter to deal with all these bulbs just in pots and pans, but quite impossible individually. Thus one is overwhelmed by one's own progeny, and nothing really worth while is accomplished. How can this situation be avoided?

Well, first of all do a little research. If you do you will amost invariably find that the two *Narcissus* bulbs you have in flower have already been crossed by someone else many years ago, perhaps with indifferent results. If you take the trouble to look up your proposed cross in the Data Bank, you will be quite astonished at what has already been done.

Let us pause for a moment to note just what the Data Bank is and how it can help. The Data Bank is the brainchild of Dr. Tom Throckmorton. He first conceived the idea of assembling all the pertinent data on every known daffodil cultivar and species and recording it on a computer. In order for this to be possible, he also had to devise a method of converting basic information into a form acceptable to the computer—hence the revised divisions and color coding mentioned in Chapter One. Once the method of color coding had been accepted internationally, the way was clear for the information to be encoded. This has now been done on a computer associated with the Methodist Medical Center at 1200 Pleasant Street, Des Moines, Iowa 50308. Computer printouts are available in a number of forms for a modest fee through the secretary of the American Daffodil Society. A complete printout costs about $20.00 but this price is bound to increase as the volume of information increases with the annual updates. A printout of all miniature hybrids and species can be obtained for only $5.00. Printouts provide the name of the cultivar or species, followed by the name of the seed parent and then the pollen parent and the name of the breeder if known. The type classification and color code appears next followed by the season of flowering, average height, chromosome count if known, and fertility data. "s" indicates fertile seed and "p" fertile pollen. Finally, the year of registration is given if known.

By referring to this record you will probably find that there is hardly a cross which has not been tried by someone else at some time or another. If the results were good the progeny will be listed if they were worth registering. But perhaps the results were indifferent, or the cross did not take and no seed was produced. Why was this? Perhaps at the time of the cross the flowers were not in the right condition, perhaps the surrounding air was too dry—any number of factors can account for an apparent failure. So, if the cross seems to be desirable then perhaps you should attempt it again under better controlled conditions.

To illustrate this point let us consider the history of 'Tete-a-Tete,' one of the most successful and satisfactory miniatures ever produced. A. W. Tait, a keen collector and grower of daffodils living in Portugal, had growing in his garden both the species N. cyclamineus and the old hybrid 'Soleil d' Or' It is not known whether he made a planned cross between these two and if so which was the seed parent. But eventually a bulb appeared in his garden which was clearly a cross between the two. It was named 'Cyclataz.' Bulbs of 'Cyclataz' were sent to Alec Gray who found it a pleasant plant, slow to increase, and quite useless as a parent for seed was never set. Then as Gray describes it, "We had one of those exceptional years when all sorts of things produced seed and in that year I found one capsule on 'Cyclataz' from which three bulbs were raised. These three were named 'Quince,' 'Jumblie' and 'Tete-a-Tete' and of the three, 'Tete-a-Tete' is by far the best." The lesson to be learned here is to never give up, because the coming year, or the next day may just be that one in which the cross you have in mind will prove successful. Notwithstanding the 'Tete-a-Tete' story, one of the most important factors in successful hybridizing remains the choice of the two parent plants. Each of them should be outstanding in some way. Two good or exceptional parents are more likely to produce outstanding offspring—it's as simple as that.

Having decided to make a cross, what should you do? Two tools are required for the actual procedure. They are a small, camel hair paint brush as used by water color artists, and a pair of dentist's tweezers with thin, pointed, curved ends. I use the thin curved tweezers most, for it is relatively easy to remove one anther from a flower with the fine point, and then gently rub it on the tip of the stigma of the other flower. If I plan to use one flower as the pollen parent for a number of crosses, then the fine brush is more useful. The brush is carefully twirled among the anthers on more than one flower of the same kind. Once the brush is fully charged with pollen it can be used to dab pollen on a number of flowers selected as female parents.

When making a cross it is usual, but not essential, to make a reciprocal cross with both flowers, using each as both the pollen and seed parent. The differences between these crosses will be slight, but occasionally a cross will take more readily one way than the other. Try both while you are at it.

The mechanics of cross pollination are really very simple. As most growers know, each flower has both male and female parts. The male parts are called anthers and are usually grouped around the center of the flower. When a flower first opens the anthers may be tightly closed but as the flowers develop, the anthers open along one side releasing a mass of yellow grains, pollen. When the anthers open up in this way the pollen is usually in a suitable condition to use. Directly in the center of each flower and usually surrounded by the anthers is a single stiff

Making a new hybrid. Select form of *Narcissus triandrus,* left. Narcissus 'Pequineta', right. Hybrid produced by crossing these, center.

Closeup of new hybrid, unnamed and under number. Cross made March 1982. First flower seen March 1986.

upright stem with a small, flat pad on the top. This is called the stigma. The stem below the pad is known as the style, and at the bottom of the style right in the depths of the flower or sometimes right behind it is a small, oval, green swelling which is the ovary containing the embryo seeds. The ovary, style and stigma together comprise the female organs.

For fertilization to take place the pollen must be in a suitable condition to transfer from the anther to the stigma at the tip of the style. The stigma must also be in a receptive state, i.e. slightly sticky, so that the pollen grains will adhere to the surface. The receptivity of the stigma develops slowly after the flower opens, but may be delayed or even aborted by atmospheric or other environmental conditions. A hot, dry spell can dry up the surface of the stigma so quickly that it remains receptive for literally only minutes. On the other hand the temperature can be so low that the necessary pre-conditioning of both pollen and stigma are never really completed. Happily the receptiveness or otherwise of flowers grown under control in a cool greenhouse can quickly be determined. Usually it is obvious whether the pollen is sticking or not and if it does changes can quickly be noted.

When fertilization has taken place, the ovary will begin to swell and the scape elongate. As the green ovary develops, the flower dies, and as the scape elongates the fat pods are held well above the foliage. Watch the pods as they develop and when they begin to turn yellow they should be gathered into a small envelope which should be clearly marked with the two parents, putting the seed-bearing parent first. I gently squeeze the pods to encourage the seeds to fall out. When empty the seed capsule is discarded. Some early crosses that might have been made before Christmas will mature first, probably by early March, but crosses are not usually complete, with ripe seed, until late April, which, even so, is much earlier than any crosses made in the open.

Once all seed has been gathered and cleaned, I then sow it, usually sometime early in May. The compost used for sowing is the same as used for potting, but bulked up with equal parts of coarse gritty sand. The sowing mix is therefore much more sandy, because I find that germination is excellent in this type of mixture. One quart plastic containers are my standard. These are about the same size as a 4 in. (10 cm) pot. The seed is sown evenly on the pot surface, covered lightly with the same sandy mixture, which in turn is covered with a light layer of pure grit. This seems to greatly reduce the formation of moss on the surface of the pots. After labelling with a number and the year plus details of the cross, the pots are placed outside in a shaded and sheltered area to spend the summer in the open.

An occasional watering is given if things get too hot and dry. Germination usually commences in late August, beginning with the more precocious *bulbocodium* types. Germination will be spasmodic right on through the winter, for any crosses which may have a *pseudonarcissus* type as one of the parents may not be seen until early spring. Ultimately most pots should have a small group of thin, grass-like seedlings. These should be kept moist but not overwatered. I always sow whatever seed I gather, because I have been pleasantly surprised to obtain seedlings from sowings of not more than one or two seeds, classed as poor and doubtful when gathered. No matter how poor the seed looks, give it a chance for at least one year.

When the seedlings are well up and before the first frost, the pots are brought into the greenhouse and placed in a remote corner of the bench. They have to take their chances with large pots of freesias and similar items which also have to be there through the winter. After Christmas, all pots receive one, weak, liquid fertilizing and a watering with Benlate to prevent fungus problems.

In late spring the pots are taken outside and allowed to die down in a normal manner. They remain untouched through the summer, apart from a few occasional waterings, but when new growth begins in the autumn the pots are plunged in a peat-perlite mix in a tight frame. This in turn is very slightly heated with an electric cable which comes on only when the weather is really severe. The tops of the pots may be slightly frozen, but heavy freezing of the total pot ball cannot be allowed.

Growth in the second year will follow the lines of the first, but the foliage will be stronger, and many bulbs will produce two or three leaves. This is particularly true of many of the bulbocodiums, for it is possible to have one or two flowers on some of these in the third season. With this possibility in mind all pots are carefully sorted over at the end of the second growing season and any large bulbs selected for potting into 4–5 in. (10–12 cm) pots in new soil. These are marked with the original number, while the small bulbs are repotted back into the plastic containers using the normal potting mix. These return to the frame for yet another year while the larger bulbs are plunged in the bench in the greenhouse along with the standard bulbs. When and if they bloom, it is easy to judge their potential qualities.

Two year old seedlings.

Although I now have many hundreds of bulbs of flowering size from earlier crossings, I have yet to see one that I think is outstanding. Many are interesting, but none exceptional. It is very easy to persuade oneself that a particular seedling is unique because you have produced it. Generally speaking, if you are honest, it is not. So be stern and critical with your progeny, and keep for further evaluation only those one or two which do suggest something different.

Once having reached this stage one has but to repeat and repeat and repeat. The limiting factors will be first, room, and second, the desire and ability to grow as many bulbs as possible as individuals until their true value can be seen. For most people space is likely to run out first. I tend to look for an interesting flower when the cross blooms for the first time. If nothing appears then I will watch for perhaps a second year and if nothing exceptional turns up, the pot of seedlings is planted out to take its chance in the prepared border. Many die, but a bulb here and there which stands out from the others is marked and returned to pan culture for further evaluation. A fine flower is not the only point of value. A really strong bulb with a robust constitution may well be a better plant for the average gardener, than a weak bulb with poor constitution chosen because it has unusual flower form or color.

Practically all the species will cross with each other once—a first cross (F1). But not all the seedlings produced are fertile for further crossings. This is particularly true of seedlings produced by crossing any form of *N. triandrus* or *N. jonquilla* with a bulb from another division. A jonquil crossed with another jonquil will produce seedlings which are usually fertile and can therefore be used to make a second cross (F2). But any bulbs which result from the *N. triandrus* with *N. jonquilla* will be sterile. Information as to compatability and viability of pollen is usually available as part of the information provided by the Daffodil Data Bank.

Storage of Pollen

If a species or cultivar flowers very early it is quite a simple matter to collect pollen and store it for use later in the season when other types are in bloom. Thus it becomes possible to make a cross between daffodils which might never meet under natural conditions.

Some fairly large, gelatin capsules should be obtained from your local pharmacist. At the same time ask him if he will save some of the small packets of dehydrators that are part of every shipment of drugs. These are either small sachets or equally small tubes containing a dehydrating chemical.

Using the curved, pointed tweezers, anthers covered with pollen are carefully removed and placed inside the capsule. If the anthers are in good condition with plenty of ripe pollen, the inside of the capsule will quickly become coated with pollen. Ideally, the capsule should become bright yellow, colored by the pollen on the inside. The capsule is then closed and placed in an empty plastic film container—the type used for new 35 mm film. The name of the narcissus from which the pollen was taken, together with one of the dehydrating sachets, is placed inside and closed. The containers are in turn put into a large plastic bag which is stored at the back of the middle shelf of an ordinary refrigerator, where the temperature will remain at about 40°F (4°C) or slightly lower. It should be obvious to the reader that only one kind of pollen can be stored in any container. Pollen gathered and stored in this way will keep for some months. When needed, the capsule is removed, and the loose pollen transferred to the stigma of the flower to be pollinated. The camel hair brush can be used if you wish to put the pollen on a number of flowers, or the broad end of a wooden toothpick can be used for more delicate application. You can even insert the stigma into the capsule if careful, and rub a little pollen from the side directly onto the stigma.

It is rather unlikely that if you become involved with hybridizing you will produce a world-beater. Such a stroke of good fortune comes to very few growers. But you may well produce a bulb which is better than the standard, or a modest improvement on either parent. This in itself is an achievement and once you have begun, these rewards will be more than sufficient to keep you dabbing pollen each spring with renewed vigor and abandon.

CHAPTER FIVE

Pests and Diseases

Daffodils as a group are not subject to any very serious pests or diseases, although the narcissus eelworm was sufficiently deadly before a suitable treatment was found a few years ago, to seriously endanger commercial daffodil growing throughout the world. But in the main, most of the really troublesome problems have been studied and some measure of control established. The one exception is the group of viruses which are responsible for many of the stripe diseases. For these, rogueing—digging and destroying all bulbs showing symptoms—is essential if stocks are to be kept clean.

A most excellent publication titled *Diseases of Narcissus.* Extension Bulletin #709, published by the Cooperative Extension Service, College of Agriculture, Washington State University, Pullman, WA 91164, covers the needs of both hobbyist and commercial grower. Diseases are illustrated in color and methods of control recommended. It is an excellent publication. Suggestions for materials to be used for the control of the major diseases are given in a separate bulletin, which is continually updated as new materials are tested and become available.

PESTS

Slugs and Snails

These are a nuisance rather than a threat. They both seem to delight in feeding upon newly opened blooms, especially if they are small and in pans. A number of proprietary slug baits are available, and any one placed down well in advance of flowering will reduce the problem to modest proportions. If the greenhouse is cleaned well before the pans are installed, and if the pans are cleaned as well, the problem will not be acute.

Narcissus Eelworm

Time was when this was an extremely serious disease which threatened all bulb growing, and in fact wiped out many stocks. The disease can be confused with stripe for the initial foliage symptoms can be very similar.

The best control for this disease is hot water treatment and the Washington State Bulletin previously mentioned gives information and clear diagrams for the construction of an effective, simple, and inexpensive hot water treatment unit. This treatment, if applied correctly, will eliminate the nematodes which cause the disease and will at the same time control a wide range of other problems such as the narcissus bulb fly, aphids, mites, plus many fungi including the fusarium responsible for basal rot. There is therefore a good argument for treating bulbs every two or three years this way.

The development of the hot water treatment technique at the R.H.S. Garden, Wisley, provided complete control of most of the problems associated with daffodil growing, and every good commercial grower now treats his stock, and will only deal in stocks which have been so treated. As a result most commercial sources are now virtually free of eelworm. It is now a rare problem unless it has inadvertently been brought in on some carelessly grown stock.

Recent tests have shown that treatment of growing plants with a good nematocide also controls eelworm, although having little effect upon the other problems. Again the latest information is to be had by writing to the Extension Service at Washington State University.

The Narcissus Fly

This is the only other pest that may be troublesome. The fly on the wing in late spring—May to June—appears rather like a large hover fly, but with a distinctive humming sound as it flies past. Eggs are laid on the ground close to dying foliage. As the grubs develop, they make their way down into the soil, closely following the line of the dying tube of leaves. Once the bulb is reached, the grubs burrow in, usually through the root plate and then quietly develop within the bulb through the following winter and spring.

A physical barrier can be provided if the dying foliage is removed and the soil raked over so that no enticing hole is visible. A heavy dressing of powdered Sevin will discourage the development of the grubs but it has a rather short effective life so may have to be repeated. Spectracide is somewhat more effective as is Cygon or Cygon E. These chemicals are generally available and regular treatments during the critical period when the fly is on the wing will reduce the problem to an item of lesser importance.

DISEASES

Basal Rot

Here is where the amateur grower may well run into trouble. The most widespread disease is Basal Rot, caused by the organism *Fusarium oxysporum* forma *narcissi,* a specific form confined to narcissus. Other forms attack iris and tulips. Some bulbs are much more susceptible than others to the disease, so if one wishes to grow these particular species or cultivars, greater care will be needed to do so successfully.

The disease is worldwide, and is found in most soils, but it is particularly prevalent in soils which have already grown a crop of narcissus. Poorly drained soils which can become water logged, together with high temperatures, can also activate the disease. While *Fusarium* is active at quite low temperatures, i.e. down to 47°F (8°C) it becomes highly active and even virulent in moist soils which reach a temperature of 85°F (30°C). A combination of hot moist weather coupled with inadequate drainage usually brings serious problems.

The hot water treatment is an excellent control particularly if formaldehyde is added to the water. The Washington State Bulletin advises growers to lift stocks where basal rot is a problem every three or four years and treat them in this way. But this may be beyond both the capacity and the inclination of an amateur gardener, particularly one who is growing many types of miniature bulbs in pans.

What can be done in such a situation? At the risk of being considered tiresome, I repeat the admonition to maintain strict "kitchen cleanliness." Clean everything including the soil in which you intend to plant, whether it be a prepared compost for pan culture or a border in the garden. Start off with everything as clean and sterile as can be obtained using reasonable methods.

Next, a great deal can be done by carefully treating the bulbs at certain periods in their handling. Infection typically develops when the bulbs are lifted and during storage. If possible bulbs should be lifted before the soil becomes too warm. Lift carefully so as not to damage the bulbs. Remove all soil and dead roots as soon as dry: if you can choose a dry period, this is a great help. Finally the bulbs should be dipped in a standard Benlate solution, i.e. 2 level tablespoons of 50% Benlate to each gallon of water. (approximately 2 gm per l.), allowed to soak for 30 minutes, and removed and dried as rapidly as possible. If the bulbs are placed into net plastic bags as they are lifted and cleaned, they can be processed and set out to dry with the minimum of trouble. Once dry the bulbs should be stored in a cool dry area until planting time. If basal rot has been a problem, or if the bulbs are new stock obtained from a source which might be contaminated, then all bulbs should again be dipped in the same manner immediately before planting. They need not be dried out this time, but can be removed from the Benlate solution and planted immediately.

As an alternative to this liquid dip treatment I have devised another method which is particularly suitable for small quantities, small bulbs, and for the culture of these bulbs in pans, a "shotgun" powder of four different fungicides, as follows:

> 4 parts by volume of 50% Benlate
> 1 part by volume of 30% Truban
> 1 part by volume of 30% Captan
> 1 part by volume of 10% Phygon

These are mixed thoroughly by sifting through a fine sieve and the powder is stored in a tight, screw top plastic container into which have been placed 3–4 of the small dehydrators mentioned earlier in reference to the storage of pollen. This fungicide mixture is slightly deliquescent—absorbs water—and can become sticky if not kept dry with the dehydrators. I do not claim any particular virtue for this mix. On the contrary I think that any combination of available fungicides, excepting that the mix should always contain Benlate, can work as well. The idea is to apply a shotgun treatment which will discourage a fairly wide spectrum of fungus problems.

I use this powder as a general treatment on all bulbs when planting, whether they are old and clean stock of my own, or new stock of doubtful cleanliness. As a pan is planted, each bulb is dipped into the powder and the root plate covered with a good layer. It is then placed on the bed of compost in the pan. Quite heavy amounts of powder will adhere, yet no harm will result. Treatment of bulbs in this way can, I believe, greatly reduce the danger of infection at the time when infection is most likely. As the new roots develop and push through the root plate into the soil, small surface lesions are made and these wounds, although quite small, can provide a point of entry and thus allow the fungus to penetrate the bulb. A heavy layer of powder seems to help prevent this type of infection.

Certain species and some cultivars are known to be particularly susceptible, and high on the list are *N. triandrus* and its derivatives. They may grow well, flower, and then suddenly fall apart just as you think you have a fine pan of strongly growing bulbs. For problem bulbs of this type I have a still more stringent regime. First of course the Benlate dip. Then at least 20% more grit is added to the growing compost to ensure first class aeration and drainage. Finally when the bulbs are being planted, I cover the drainage hole with a crock and half fill the pan with the new gritty mixture. This is levelled, then I add a thin layer, about ¼ in. (6 mm) of pure grit. On top of this is sprinkled a generous dressing of the fungicide powder described above. The bulbs are rolled in this fungicide powder until they are completely covered and then placed in position on the layer of grit. The bulbs are covered with more plain grit so that they are finally completely surrounded by grit. A final sprinkling of fungicide powder is then applied to the top of the grit, after which the pan is filled with compost to the required level. I have found that actually maintaining the body of the bulbs in this layer of grit greatly reduces and in time eliminates the problem of basal rot on difficult bulbs.

There is clear evidence that the incidence of this disease is reduced through the constant use of this method of planting. I have stocks which in their first year might experience at least a 10% mortality rate. Clean them and plant them as described, and next year the loss may be down to 5% and ultimately settle down to a maximum of 1% or less. Just as this disease, in fact any disease, can slowly build up under sloppy conditions, so can the problem be steadily reduced by added care, but it does take time.

Once the crop is under way great care must be taken not to over-water. It is very easy to do, and this is one reason why I now plunge all my pans, as plunging evens out the rate of water loss from all pans, no matter what their size. Water very occasionally, and only when you can see that the medium surrounding the pans is becoming dry. Then attempt to direct your watering as much as possible to the plunging medium between the pans rather than onto the pots. Some water is bound to fall upon the pot surface, but if you keep this to the minimum and largely limit the water to the space between the pots, the water will ultimately be drawn through the pot into the growing medium. The only exception to this rule occurs when all the plants are in full growth, and a hot day appears which clearly indicates the need to water everything well. But such an occasion is rare, and the exception rather than he rule.

Botrytis

As the growing season progresses, a close watch must be kept on the growth of all bulbs and any that display stunted or yellow leaves should be closely examined. The cause may be basal rot, stripe disease or possibly botrytis. Doubtful specimens should be carefully lifted from the pan with a long bladed knife, and if necessary, destroyed. How can you tell which is which? Bulbs infested with basal rot usually have a weak root system and feel rather soft. Destroy them. Bulbs infested with stripe may be quite well rooted but the leaves will tend to twist, and under a clear bright light, lighter streaks down the foliage can easily be observed. Destroy these also. Botrytis infection may be confined to a narrow area at the neck of the bulb, the bases only of a few leaves being diseased, while one or two in the center remain apparently healthy. These may be saved.

There is no question that with the first two problems, the bulbs should be discarded, but if a bulb appears to have botrytis and is valuable, it can sometimes be saved by carefully peeling off any infected outer layers and then soaked in a solution of Subdue. This is an extremely potent fungicide developed by Ciba-Geigy and marketed as a liquid under the name Subdue 2E. It is a specific for forms of *Phytophthora* and *Pithium*. The standard treatment requires only ½ fl. oz. (15 ml to 378 l) of water which works out at about 1½ ccs per gallon (3.78 l). At this strength it can be used on most plants as a soil drench applied to any pan where problems occur.

The diseased bulbs are first removed and then the soil surrounding them is soaked with Subdue, which is applied whether the pan actually requires water or not. If the disease is well advanced, one or perhaps two adjacent bulbs may have become infected, but regular use of the Subdue solution substituted for normal watering will ultimately halt the advance of the disease. If a bulb is to be saved, soak it for 30 minutes and then replant in fresh sandy compost in a clean pot, where it may reroot and recover. I make such an effort only if a bulb is of some value, for it is not a method for routine use. But Subdue used to halt the spread of disease in a pan of good bulbs is of real value, so I always have it on hand for this purpose. It is essentially a commercial material designed for large scale use on nurseries and it is quite expensive. But such small quantities are needed that the pint which I have had on hand for some years is still more than ⅔s full. A pipette or a graduated dropper is necessary to measure out the 1.5 ccs needed for each gallon.

The steady application of good clean growing practices, the regular treatment of all bulbs as planted, plus the spot treatment of infected areas in a pan from which diseased bulbs have been removed has, over a four year period, so reduced the virulence of basal rot, that if I now find more than four or five infected bulbs in a growing stock of well over 3,000 I begin to worry. Continual care of this kind brings this and related diseases within manageable proportions.

Botrytis can be a problem with small daffodils in a greenhouse. It may appear as a grey mould on the yellowing end of leaves as they are dying down, on faded flowers which have not been removed, and is occasionally the cause of premature yellowing of foliage, a symptom which is easily confused with the first signs of basal rot. You can be fairly certain that it is botrytis if the bulb, when lifted, has a full and apparently clean root system. A botrytis attack on the base of the leaves just at or below ground level is the most likely suspect. Botrytis requires a fairly warm and above all moist atmosphere to develop, so it can usually be controlled by increasing ventilation to keep the air buoyant and continually in motion. If a ventilating fan is used rather than sky lights, the controls should be set down, especially on still and stagnant days, so that the fan runs even if the air temperature is quite low, say 45°F (7°C). Air movement will ensure that the tops of the bulbs remain dry and so prevent the onset of the disease. If despite these measures the disease does appear, the answer is first to ventilate more, and second to spray or drench with Subdue.

Stripe

This last disease is the most difficult because there really is no cure. The cause is a virus which may be any one of 18 viruses known to infect *Narcissus*. Among the worst is narcissus yellow stripe, which is quite prevalent and can cause heavy damage. The initial symptom is the appearance of light green to yellow stripes on the leaves and flower stems, followed by stunting and distortion of the development of both. As soon as this striping is noticed, usually quite early in the season, the bulbs should be carefully lifted and destroyed. This rogueing is practiced by both commercial and amateur growers wishing to keep their stocks clean.

The virus is usually transmitted by aphids so spraying or fumigating to control aphids while growth is active is a first class way of limiting the spread. Because many of the jonquil types remain green much later in the spring, when aphids are more prevalent and active, many of these bulbs have become badly infected, to the point that virus-free stocks appear to be unobtainable. The only solution then is to return to production by seed, which is slow but nevertheless practical in the case of the species, or to tissue culture for the cultivars. This last is a highly technical procedure, and as such outside the scope of this book. I have noted that at times, bulbs growing indoors in pans will produce what appears to be striped foliage, but when the bulbs are planted outside the symptoms seem to disappear. It is perhaps more accurate to say that the symptoms are masked by the deeper green of the foliage when the bulbs are grown outside. So if you can bring yourself to do it—as you should—remove all doubtful bulbs as they begin to grow, and destroy them. You will lose a few bulbs but the remainder will be much safer from infection.

To sum up for all forms of stripe: First remove and destroy all doubtful bulbs; second control aphids by regular spraying; third, dig stocks as early as possible to limit the time the foliage is at risk.

Section Two
Species and Hybrids

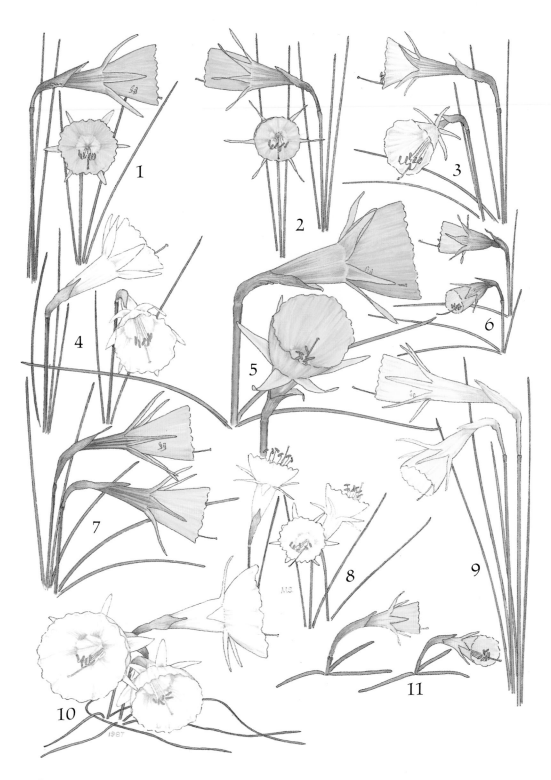

Plate 1. 1, *Narcissus bulbocodium* subsp. *bulbocodium*; 2, *N. bulbocodium* var. *conspicuus*; 3, *N. bulbocodium* var. *graellsii*; 4, *N. cantabricus* subsp. *cantabricus*; 5, *N. bulbocodium* subsp. *obesus*; 6, *N. bulbocodium* subsp. *tenuifolius*; 7, *N. bulbocodium* subsp. *citrinus*; 8, *N. bulbocodium* subsp. *albidus* (*N. tananicus* of trade); 9, *N. cantabricus* var. *foliosus*; 10, *N. cantabricus* var. *clusii*.

CHAPTER SIX

The Bulbocodiums

"What's in a name? That which we call a rose by any other name
would smell as sweet."

What Shakespeare said about a rose—and he seemed to have something to say about most things—applies equally well to daffodils. Whether we like it or not, and for esoteric reasons not usually clear to the typical gardener, a well-loved plant, known and appreciated for years under one name may suddenly be given a new name. Example: a winter flowering iris, native to Algeria and other countries bordering on the Mediterranean, used to be known as *Iris stylosa.* The bunch of wiry green leaves turn into gray straw with the onset of winter. Then early in February, quite large, typical iris flowers appear on short stems from the midst of the straw. Fragrant and of a pale lavender-blue, the flowers are a delight if picked and brought indoors at a time when flowers of any kind are few. But if you look through modern plant catalogs for *Iris stylosa* you cannot find it, for now it is listed as *Iris unguicularis*—a horrible name, difficult to pronounce and not at all indicative of the real style which the plant most certainly possesses.

This changing of names has struck the genus *Narcissus* especially hard with the publication of the new *Flora Europaea* and as a result many of the fine old names under which we have acquired, grown and enjoyed many bulbous species have been swept away. We are told that the bulbs in the various sections are so closely related, that it is difficult and indeed unwise to attempt to distinguish between them.

The problem lies mainly in the fact that many of these species are infinitely variable in the wild. If a plant explorer enters a valley with a substantial population of, shall we say, *N. bulbocodium,* he could discover individuals which closely resemble almost all of the so-called forms to which individual names have been given in the past. The inference was, by using these names, that the forms known as *N. bulbocodium* var. *nivalis* was a clearly defined variety of the basic *N. bulbocodium.* However, knowledgeable growers such as John Blanchard, who have seen most of these bulbs in the wild, collected them and grown them, will say that there just is no "typical form."

Certainly *N. bulbocodium* var. *nivalis* is a first class example. As I write, my collection of bulbs under this name is coming into bloom. There are six pans, each representing different collections from the wild. Each appears to be superficially the same, yet they are not, particularly in size and height of flowers. All the flowers have more or less the same general form associated with this name, i.e. the corona is much longer than it is wide and the flowers develop directly at right angles to the stem. The color is a bright chrome yellow, and the stems are 3–4 in. (7.5–10 cm) high emerging from the middle of a tuft of stiff, upright, dark green leaves. Yet none of these six are the same. First they range widely in height of stem, the largest being perhaps 8 in. (20 cm) tall, with a flower larger than the others. A "giant" *nivalis* in fact. Another lot is equally diminutive, with stems not more than 3 in. (7.5 cm) tall and a flower size to match. Which is the "true" *N. bulbocodium* var. *nivalis?* I have come to the conclusion that in these matters John Blanchard is correct, there simply is no typical form of any of the wild species in certain sections.

When discussing this matter with friends, I was told that if a pan purporting to represent a species or subspecies is shown, it may be questioned if the pan is obviously a clone, i.e. a number of bulbs, all exactly the same, clearly increased by division. Because they are all the same, even if the form is excellent, they cannot be representative of the bulb as found in the wild. Any pan or collection which sets out to be representative of a species or subspecies should contain plants all very similar but differing slightly in minor ways. I can see the reasoning behind this position, yet as a grower and collector of plants, and more especially as a nurseryman, this view goes against the grain. Most keen growers of any plant, be they amateur or professional, always have a watchful eye open at all times for the appearance of something good, better, or unusual which might justify segregating the individual and propagating it vegetatively to produce a clone. If with further experience this clone maintains its superior qualities, then it surely must have its own name. It is this kind of watchfulness by keen plantsmen which has given us a multitude of superior plants throughout horticulture.

In an effort to find some compromise between the botanist and the plantsman I propose to follow the general outline of the *Flora Europaea,* as set out and interpreted by John Blanchard in his paper of 1981, and published in the Daffodil Yearbook of the R.H.S. in 1981–82. But names which we have used in the past will be given as varietal names rather than subspecies.

Narcissus bulbocodium, the so called "hoop petticoat" daffodil, is found in one form or another over the entire native geographic range for narcissus, from southern France to Morocco. Everyone is agreed that this is one of the most difficult sections to classify because, to quote John Blanchard, "They come in a bewildering range of shapes, sizes and colors."

There are two main groups which overlap slightly. The first includes all the species and subspecies found in Europe, the second, very similar and clearly closely related, are those bulbs found in North Africa. Let us turn to the European section first.

This group can again be divided into two sections, those with yellow, citron or pale yellow flowers, and those with white flowers. The main species in the yellow group is *N. bulbocodium,* found, in one form or another. throughout Spain, Portugal, and into southern France. The flowers range from a pale to a deep chrome yellow, the most typical form being that which we know as *N. bulbocodium* var. *conspicuus.* Under this heading we must also now include forms previously known as: *N.b.* var. *citrinus* N.b. var. *filifolius,* N.b. var. *tenuifolius,* N.b. var. *nivalis.* N.b. var. *graellsii,* N.b. var. *vulgaris* and perhaps *N.b.* var. *genuinus* and *N.b.* var. *serotinus.* Now let us see if we can sort this lot out.

N. bulbocodium subsp. *bulbocodium* var. *conspicuus.* 10 Y-Y.

I have placed this variety first because it is the bulb most commonly available and grown by gardeners everywhere. Most of the material offered in garden stores to date is collected material from either Spain or Portugal, and as such, can vary considerably. However, this is about to change for new rules have effectively banned the importation of collected material, and so from 1987 most bulbs will either be grown domestically, or in the Netherlands. Typically the bulb is quite hardy, producing strong bunches of thin, upright leaves in a dense tuft, perhaps 10–12 in. (25–30 cm) high. The flowers are produced on 8–10 in. (20–25 cm) stems, one flower per stem. The corona is a typical goblet shape and should be a deep, clear yellow, although some types can be found with a number of green stripes down the outside. The flowers should be of a fair size with the corona perhaps ¾ in. (2 cm) long and 1 in. (2.5 cm) wide. It is an easy bulb to grow, and does not appear to be susceptible to any of the diseases such as basal rot, which cause real problems with other species. Grown in pans in the greenhouse the bulbs will commence flowering in late February and on into March, or about a month later out of doors. This is a thoroughly satisfying bulb to grow in a raised miniature border.

There are many forms of this bulb in cultivation, some much better than others. As mentioned earlier, stock being offered for sale now is almost certain to be commercially grown, and in most instances a clone. These all flower well and are quite hardy.

Selected Forms of *N. bulbocodium* subsp. *bulbocodium* var. *conspicuus*.

Form No. 1. Originally collected and then grown in a nursery so this may still retain the many small variations in both morphology and performance.

Form No. 2. This is clearly a selection and so a clone. I obtained this from a grower in England, and the stock is completely uniform.
The bulb is slightly smaller and the foliage not so strong. The stems are perhaps 7–8 in. (17 to 20 cm) long and the flower color a rich, deep gold. The corona is a fine, wide open goblet, even, and of good size. It blooms heavily either in pans or outdoors. An excellent selection.

Form No. 3. A further selection with the edge of the corona deeply frilled. It grows as well as the others, flowers heavily and is a most attractive bulb. A clone.

Narcissus bulbocodium var. *conspicuus*. The typical form.

*Narcissus
bulbocodium* var.
conspicuus.
Frilled form.

*Narcissus
bulbocodium* var.
citrinus. Form
growing in the
lawn, Savill
Gardens.

N. bulbocodium **subsp.** *bulbocodium* **var.** *citrinus.* **10 Y-Y.**

Although this variant has to be considered as part of the *conspicuus* group, practically every *bulbocodium,* whether European or African, can be found in a pale yellow form, usually with green overtones from the sepals. Should all be called var. *citrinus?* The most common form and one well known to bulb lovers everywhere is that which grows so profusely in the lawns of the Savill Gardens and on the alpine meadow at Wisley, in England. I prefer to think of this as the standard type. It flowers quite early in February under glass and in mid-March outside. The flowers are of an average size on 6 in. (15 cm) stems, with a fairly wide-open, cone-shaped corona. The color is pale yellow, with a distinct greenish tinge as the flowers first open. In some the green cast is accentuated by a distinct green stripe down the outside of the perianth tube. It grows easily, seeds freely, and obviously naturalizes well in grass.

N. bulbocodium **subsp.** *bulbocidium* **var.** *citrinus* **forma 'Landes'.**

A bulb under the name of *N. bulbocodium* var. *citrinus* 'Landes' was collected from an area near Bayonne, France, and recorded as being of exceptional size. Described and illustrated in the 1938 *Daffodil Yearbook,* it was noted as being similar to the standard *bulbocodium* but with much larger flowers.

The group of bulbs I received were seedlings and as might be expected many variations in both color and form appeared among the group. The flowers are considerably larger than any other form, and colors range from a pale yellow, through a medium yellow to one with a pale yellow, slightly tinged with green. A strong green stripe extends down the side of the perianth tube.

When mature all the bulbs throw multiple buds, four, five, and even six from a bulb and thus can produce a brave show of flowers. Individual flowers may be 2 in. (5 cm) across and quite outstanding. All are first class growers, opening in mid-February in pans under glass. While the plain yellow form falls neatly into the *conspicuus* category, the pale yellow with green stripe appears to be a first class form of *citrinus.* All these bulbs are being grown, individually as clones.

Narcissus bulbocodium forma 'Landes'. Showing differences between seedlings.

N. bulbocodium subsp. bulbocodium var. filifolius. 10 Y-Y.

Alec Gray in one of his catalogs notes that this is so close to *N. bulbocodium* var. *conspicuus* that he intended to lump them together. The form that I have under this name is clearly distinct and is presumably a selection, vegetatively propagated, and therefore a clone. The foliage, as the name suggests, is quite fine, much finer than the type, and abundant. Foliage appears early, and because it is thin, quickly becomes almost prostrate. Yet the bulb does not flower until March, even when grown in pans in a cool greenhouse. Of medium height—6–7 in. (15–17 cm)—the flowers are a smooth goblet of bright yellow, which develop to the point that a pan of bulbs becomes a round, yellow orb of color when all are open. It is exceptionally good and an excellent bulb in every way.

Narcissus bulbocodium var. *filifolius.*

N. bulbocodium subsp. bulbocodium var. genuinus. 10 Y-Y.

There seems to be some doubt as to this name. Jefferson-Brown, in his 1951 book *The Daffodil*, lists it as *N. bulbocodium* subsp. *vulgaris* forma *genuinus*. The 1966 Daffodil Handbook of the American Horticultural Society describes it as a form of *N. bulbocodium* var. *conspicuus* with a distribution in Spain and Portugal. Last year I received bulbs collected at Marrakesh in Morocco under this name from Michael Salmon, and in the 1986–7 edition of the *Daffodil Yearbook*, in an excellent review of narcissus in North Africa, he states that it is found in modest numbers on acid slopes at 6,500 ft. (1,950 m) in the Middle and High Atlas mountains.

The bulbs which I received from him have since flowered with quite large

Narcissus bulbocodium var. *genuinus*.

flowers of a clear, light yellow. The corona is distinctly larger than the typical *N. bulbocodium* var. *conspicuus* and more closely resembles a form of *N. bulbocodium* collected many years ago in southern France, near Landes.

This is a good bulb which grows without difficulty, and produces excellent flowers of an unusual size.

N. bulbocodium subsp. *bulbocodium* var. *graellsii.* 10 Y-Y.

The only virtue possessed by this bulb is that it is the last *bulbocodium* to bloom. The plant is also peculiar in that it appears to have no clear-cut period of dormancy, for the leaves remain green right on into the summer. It starts to bloom in mid-April for me and continues spasmodically for some time. The flowers are not outstanding, being of moderate size and pale yellow.

It is of interest mainly to a collector, and might be of value if one wished to produce a group of hybrids which flowered much later than the standard varieties. I have also found it to be moderately susceptible to basal rot, so care is needed with watering.

N. bulbocodium subsp. *bulbocodium* var. *nivalis.* 10 Y-Y.

This is a very small plant both in stature and in flower. The foliage is usually stiff, upright, and not more than 3–4 in. (7.5.–10 cm) high. Each bulb produces a thick tuft of leaves from which 1–5 strong buds eventually emerge. Each bud becomes a small flower of distinct shape, i.e. a long, narrow, tapered corona of bright yellow. Some coronas may be slightly flared, but generally the corona is quite long and gently tapered from a narrow base to a slightly wider cup. It is one of the first to flower in pans, sometimes producing an odd flower in December with more following in January and February. But at no time does the pan have a bright show of flowers. They seem to trickle on for upwards of three months, without producing a substantial show at any time. Some of my later acquisitions developed in the general form as described but have been much larger in all respects. This suggests that there is plenty of room for improvement by clonal selection. It is now just an interesting plant, of value mostly to the collector.

Narcissus bulbocodium var. *serotinus.*

N. bulbocodium subsp. *bulbocodium* var. *serotinus.* **10 Y-Y.**

Another name in contention. It is listed in Fernandes review of 1968 as a form of *N. bulbocodium* var. *conspicuus* coming from an area of west Portugal and flowering from March to May. Salmon reports that he found bulbs of a similar type in the High Atlas in Morocco, flowering from Christmas to early March. The name itself means "late" but the bulb I grow in pans is among the first to bloom. Last year I recorded the first flower on the 11th of November, which relates correctly to a bulb normally flowering in late December in Morocco.

The bulb is excellent, producing large, open, bowl-shaped flowers of a deep yellow. The stems are strong and from 8–10 in. (20–25 cm) tall. It does very well in pans but I have not yet tried it outside.

N. bulbocodium subsp. *bulbocodium* var. *tenuifolius.* **10 Y-Y.**

I have grown many collections reputed to be this but very few plants seem to agree with the originally published descriptions. Gray remarks that this is very close to var. *conspicuus* but has prostrate foliage. Virtually all the bulbs I have grown with prostrate foliage have produced flowers which are so small and with so narrow a corona hat I consider them to be *N. bulbocodium* var. *nivalis.* But now and

Narcissus bulbocodium var. *tenuifolius.*

then a few plants will appear which are close to *N. bulbocodium* var. *conspicuus* in color and size of flower, but with prostrate foliage. I assume these are the true *N. bulbocodium* var. *tenuifolius.* The bulbs are usually white-skinned, grow with ease, and split regularly into two or three good-sized bulbs, each also of flowering size. It may be possible to eventually establish a form corresponding closely to the original description, but when done I see no practical advantage. At best, it seems to me to be a somewhat inferior form of *N. bulbocodium* var. *conspicuus.*

N. bulbocodium obesus. **10 Y-Y.**

This is the only other species recognized by *Flora Europaea,* and as might be expected there are many forms. The basic species is quite distinct, for the foliage is rather thick, even appearing somewhat succulent as it twists horizontally over the top of the pan and down the side. Foliage is completely prostrate when mature, and if the growing medium is too rich, the mat of foliage can be an embarrassment, as it makes it difficult for the flower buds to thrust through. But under normal circumstances, bulbs in pans will develop quite a substantial area of prostrate leaves, through which the flower buds begin to emerge in mid-February. When the bulbs are strong and healthy, four, five, and up to eight buds may arise from each, the stems rising 3 in. (7.5 cm) above the leaves before the flowers open. The corona is exaggerated into a truly obese balloon, and the color is usually a clear, bright yellow. I have three forms which vary in the size of the flowers but not in general color and form. Needless to say, the form with the largest flower is the poorest grower.

Narcissus bulbocodium subsp. *obesus.* Typical form with prostrate foliage.

Narcissus bulbocodium subsp. *obesus.* Cream flowered form from seed.

But there are good forms which do very well, which brings up a point of importance with regard to almost all wild forms. Without question, there are both good and bad forms offered for sale. Thus, if one obtains bulbs under a certain name and they do not do as well as described, do not give up. Instead, look for an alternative source and order again, and again if necessary. In every instance when I have received and grown a bulb which is clearly inferior, I have been able to find, eventually, a greatly superior form of apparently the same bulb. The difference between the two can be quite extreme.

Although I know of no wild form of *obesus* which has a pale yellow color— *citrinus* type—in growing batches of seedlings I have produced a number which are clearly *obesus* in form and in a range of colors from pale yellow to white. It remains to be seen if these are as good as the type.

N. hedraeanthus

This strange little oddity is included in the Bulbocodium section as a separate species although it bears little resemblance to any of the others. The foliage tends to be quite sparse, twisted and generally prostrate. The flowers are small, tubular and with exceptionally exerted anthers. They are even smaller than *N. bulbocodium* subsp. *bulbocodium,* var. *nivalis.* The stems are short, usually not more than 1 in. (2.5 cm) or at the most, 2 in. (5 cm). In pans the bulbs commence to flower in early January and continue on into February. Generally they are a pale yellow, although I have had bulbs which flowered with a deep yellow color, but this does not seem to be stable as it can revert to the paler form. I have also flowered a pure white one. All are interesting to grow, but as an oddity only.

Narcissus hedraeanthus.

N. cantabricus **10 W-W**

This is the one white-flowered form which is native to Europe and north Africa as well. Although it clearly belongs in the Bulbocodium Section, the use of the name *bulbocodium* has been dropped, and it is given specific rank as *N. cantabricus*. Many different forms have been collected and named, and we shall consider some of these individually. However, let us first consider the basic differences which exist between forms of *N. bulbocodium* and *N. cantabricus*.

Professor Fernandes has suggested that *N. cantabricus* is distinct from *N. bulbocodium* in a number of ways, although clearly they are closely related. The main differences are these:

Bulbocodium	*Cantabricus*
1. Flowers yellow	1. Flowers white
2. External scales (skin) of the bulbs vary from whitish to dark brown.	2. External scales are always dark brown. (almost black)
3. Flowers with pedicels	3. Flowers nearly sessile.
4. Flowers slightly fragrant	4. Flowers very fragrant
5. Corona not expanded.	5. Corona expanded at throat.
6. Grows in open situations	6. Grows in shade of bushes.

In Europe, *N. cantabricus* seems to be mainly confined to areas in southern Spain, but it can also be found in adjacent areas of north Africa. In a recent review of these bulbs in north Africa. Michael Salmon explains quite clearly the differences between *N. cantabricus* and very similar bulbs also found in the same region, but with the name *N. romieuxii* subsp. *albidus*. It is very easy to confuse these two and the differences, when observed and understood are quite clear. He lists them as follows:

1. All forms of *N. cantabricus* have flowers of a particularly clear crystalline texture, and remain white as the flowers fade.
2. The rather bell-shaped appearance of the *N. cantabricus* perianth tube is quite obvious and distinct when compared with the straight-sided tube of other north African species and other variants such as *N. romieuxii* or *N. romieuxii* subsp. *albidus*.

N. cantabricus **subsp.** *cantabricus.* **10 W-W.**

There are two forms of this bulb which are presumed to be European, although exactly similar forms may be found in Morocco. These are *N. cantabricus* subsp. *monophyllus* and *N. cantibricus* var. *clusii*.

N. cantabricus **subsp.** *monophyllus.* **10 W-W.**

I am not certain that I have yet grown this variety. Alec Gray speaks most highly of it and yet most of the bulbs I have received under this name have been disappointing. Michael Salmon also speaks well of it as found in Africa, but the bulbs I have had so far have hardly been worth growing. I have three lots, all remarkably similar, with weak sparse foliage and a few flowers, equally weak. It is true that the flowers, when produced, are certainly delicate and a clear, crisp white.

I was beginning to despair and to doubt Gray's assessment when I obtained yet another lot under the same name which has lived up to its reputation in every way. It grows well, with strictly limited foliage as one might expect. In mid-January the pan is filled with upwards of 50 or more blooms on short 2–3 in. (5 to 7.5 cm) stems of a brilliant crisp white. Do not write off the form *monophylus* until you have tried, and then tried again.

Narcissus cantabricus
subsp. *monophyllus.*

N. cantabricus var. clusii. 10 W-W.

This is now not considered a valid name, for it has been submerged into the larger catch-all of *N. cantabricus* subsp. *cantabricus.* There is a published note that this form originated from a collection made in the south of France, but I doubt it. The bulb came to me under the name *clusii* and as such it exactly fits the published descriptions. The leaves are neither so tall nor so profuse as in some of the African forms, and the plant commences to grow somewhat later in the autumn. But, more importantly, it does not begin to show its buds until the end of the year, is budding well by the end of January, and comes into full flower in early February when most other forms are well over. This, of course, is under glass. The flower stems are quite short, 3–4 in. (7.5 cm). The flowers are a good size, being at least ½ in. (12.2 mm) across and have a wide, goblet-shaped cup of the purest white, held almost vertically on the stem. A pan can be completely covered with flowers when in full bloom. It is not subject to any disease problems, grows well, and is an excellent bulb, for it extends the flowering season of this white group substantially.

Narcissus cantabricus
var *clusii.*

NORTH AFRICAN FORMS OF THE BULBOCODIUM SECTION

While there is no question that the African bulbs do belong in the Section Bulbocodium, there is argument, not yet resolved, as to whether some should be given subspecies status.

Of the Bulbocodium forms already listed, specimens of *N. bulbocodium* var. *genuinus*, *N. bulbocodium* var. *nivalis*. *N. bulbocodium obesus* and *N. bulbocodium* var. *serotinus* are also to be found, more or less identical to those growing in Europe. *N. cantabricus* is also relatively common and some of the more desirable forms now in cultivation have come from the north African region.

N. cantabricus var. *foliosus*. **10 W-W.**

This is one of the very best and should be high on any grower's list of priorities when starting a collection. Over the years I have had a number of stocks, and as is true with many of the Bulbocodiums, some are clearly much better than others.

Typically the bulbs are dark brown, and of fair size, i.e. the size of an unshelled hazelnut. The leaves are produced in strong tufts, generally more or less upright, and quite dense. First buds appear early in November in the cool-house, and by mid-month some color should be seen. They are usually in full bloom by the end of November, continuing through the month of December and into January. Each stem ranges from 4–8 in. (10–20 cm) in height depending upon the form. The flower is a beautiful, full goblet-shaped corona, typically bulbocodium, and ranging in color from pale cream to a crisp white. But in the lots of bulbs I have received, flowers of many forms have been seen.

Narcissus cantabricus **var.** *foliosus.*

A recent collection which flowered for the first time in 1987 was of startling, even dazzling white and with a deeply notched edge to the corona giving the flower a truly frilled appearance. Another bulb from a different collection produced a stem at least 12 in. (50 cm) high and upon this the largest corona I have yet seen in any bulb in this species. Crisp and clear white, the bloom lasted in good condition for over three weeks. This bulb will be segregated and grown on to build up a stock, for it may well prove to be an outstanding addition.

I mention these to demonstrate that it is still possible to find bulbs growing in the wild which may be superior to any already in cultivation. This group of bulbs, good as they are, can still be considered as being at the edge of discovery, as further and more discerning collections are made. Color can range from the crispest, pristine white to a rich cream, although the latter usually fades to a near-white as the flowers age. I have segregated three forms so far which I think are sufficiently different to warrant propagation and development as clones.

N. cantabricus var. foliosus. Form #1. 10 W-W.

This form was originally segregated because it seemed to be shorter in the stem than all others. This may not be a valid reason for separating it from Form #2, for in other respects they are very similar. The flower stems on this selection are from 4–5 in. (10–13 cm) high and the flowers open creamy white which fades to white as they develop. They are of a good size, and the corona is spread wide, ½ in. (12 mm) and slightly flared with a frilled edge. The bulbs are dark brown and the foliage thin and semi-prostrate. It grows well, flowers heavily and gives no trouble.

N. cantabricus var. foliosus. Form #2. 10 W-W.

Although this is superficially very similar to Form #1, it was selected from a mixed grill of bulbs supposed to be N. bulbocodium var. mesatlanticus. The selection proved to be a happy one for the bulb has proven to be exceptionally vigorous and prolific in natural increase from division. One bulb will usually produce three or four flowers, and then split into two, three or even four bulbs, each developing into flowering size by the end of the growing season. It flowers towards the end of November with flowers very similar to Form #1, but the stems are usually at least 6 in. (15 cm) high or higher.

N. cantabricus var. foliosus. Form #3. 10 W-W.

This bulb was purchased as N. cantabricus var. clusii but it does not correspond in any way to the published description of clusii, for it is not late-flowering as N. cantabricus var. clusii is supposed to be. It flowers at the same time as the other forms of foliosus, i.e. late November and into December. It is an extremely vigorous bulb producing strong tufts of somewhat thicker leaves which remain semi-upright. From each bulb, two, sometimes three and occasionally four strong stiff stems arise, quite solid and thick as compared to others, which may eventually become from 8–10 in. (20–25 cm) high. Each stem bears a substantially larger flower than the other forms and of a clear, crisp white. In shape, the corona is less flared, being more truly goblet-shaped with a slightly wavy edge. It is on this flower in particular that one can quite clearly see the bell-shaped appearance of the perianth tube described by Michael Salmon as one of the distinguishing characteristics between forms of N. cantabricus and N. romieuxii subsp. albidus.

A pan full of these bulbs in flower is a most elegant sight. One can perhaps sum up by saying that this is a bulb with "quality" which makes it a pleasure to grow. Strong and vigorous, it is a first-class bulb, and one to which I look forward

Narcissus cantabricus var. *foliosus.* Selected form #3.

with anticipation each year. It is also an excellent pollen or seed parent, which I have used both ways in a number of crossings. I consider this one of the best.

N. cantabricus subsp. *petunioides.* 10 W-W.

This is one of the gems of this group, and when seen well grown in a pan the effect can be simply stunning. The bulb apparently originated as a single specimen segregated from a group of *N. cantabricus* received from a Dutch grower by John Blanchard's father. The bulbs now available must, therefore, be considered a clone, excepting perhaps some that have been offered which are similar and presumably are open-pollinated seedlings from the original. Dr. Fernandes considered it sufficiently different to suggest that it be considered a subspecies of *N. cantabricus* and he so lists it. The *Daffodil Handbook* of the American Horticultural Society notes, "A highly distinctive plant not yet widely available." Certainly they are true in their appraisal, for it is indeed an exceptional bulb, but happily now more generally available than it was 20 years ago.

The bulb appears very similar to the other *cantabricus* forms, with a very dark brown skin. Growth commences somewhat later than others, the first buds not usually being seen until at least mid-December. By the middle of January many blooms appear and flowering continues well into February. The foliage is not quite so dense, and the flower stems are rather short, 5–6 in. (13–15 cm) at most. As each flower opens, the wide white corona spreads until, fully extended, it becomes a flat yet frilled circle of the crispest white you can imagine. The flower is somewhat reminiscent of a petunia—hence the name. The substance of the flower—the solidity and strength of the tissues of the corona—is so firm that the widely spread

Narcissus cantabricus subsp. *petunioides*. One of the gems of the bulbocodiums.

corona, once extended, maintains its posture without drooping or wavering in any way.

Most flowers measure at least 1 ¾ in. (3.5 cm) across when fully open. A pan of this form is therefore quite an exceptional sight, and one to be eagerly anticipated. I have had no difficulty in growing this bulb for it does not seem to be any more susceptible to disease than others. However, when receiving new stock stringent precautions are desirable to ensure that the bulbs did not arrive with a built-in problem. I have had *N. cantabricus* subsp. *petunioides* for some years now yet I always accept a bulb from anyone just to check my stock. One such bulb received last year quickly languished and died after planting, while the main pan grew well.

It is noted in the literature that this variety has never been found in the wild, but I do not think this is now true. I have received bulbs newly collected in Morocco by Michael Salmon, which have flowered with the typical petunioid flower-form. The flowers were slightly smaller than the original and appear to be exactly similar to a form previously given to me by John Blanchard, which I named, for my own benefit, *N. cantabricus* var. *petunioides* "minor" I am told that this is not a valid name.

N. cantabricus var. *petunioides*. Small Form.

This plant is exactly the same as the standard *N.c. petunioides* except being slightly smaller in every way. The foliage is not so heavy and tall, the flower stems shorter, and the flowers, while being of the typical *petunioides* form are just not quite so large. I noted that my pan last year showed some buds early in December and the pan was in full bloom on January 20th. The stems are only 2 in. (5 cm) tall, but the flowers are of exceptional firmness, and a crisp, crystalline white. It increases rather slowly. My original 9 small bulbs are now 22 in four growing seasons. It can also be increased by seed. I do not think this bulb is freely available, but if you can find it, it is sure to please.

N. cantabricus var. tananicus.

Michael Salmon in his 1986 paper on the *Narcissus* of North Africa considers that the plant grown both in North America and Europe under this name is not correct. He lists it as a form of *N. albidus* and we shall consider it under that name.

N. bulbocodium var. mesatlanticus. Form #1. 10 Y-Y.

I wish I knew how these variants came to be selected and named, for, looking at them in growth and flower, it seems they could all be included under the heading *romieuxii*. Truly, I can see little difference between any of them and if a grower were to mix up two pans, I defy him to separate them. Be that as it may, we must consider them briefly, because there are one or two very good forms available here, and they will most certainly be offered under this name, at least for the time being.

The basic type has thin upright foliage in quite thick tufts. Flower buds appear in late November under glass, and flowers usually begin to open by the middle of December. The stems are 6–8 in. (15–20 cm) high and the flowers are a pale yellow, with a wide open cup or corona, usually somewhat frilled at the edge. The bulb grows well, has few problems, and performs from year to year with excellent regularity. It is a good bulb.

Narcissus bulbocodium var. *mesatlanticus.*

N. *bulbocodium* var. *mesatlanticus* Form #2. 10 Y-Y.

Very similar to Form #1 except the stems are shorter as the flowers begin to open, although they elongate later. The corona is deeply frilled, so much so that on occasions the frilling becomes an important part of the total effect. The corona is also much flatter and broader. The total effect, therefore, is quite different, although the color, habit of growth and time of flowering are similar to Form #1. This is a very dainty bulb.

N. *bulbocodium* var. *mesatlanticus,* Form #3. 10 Y-Y.

This is the form which received an Award of Merit from the R.H.S. in 1981. It is exactly the same as Form #1 in habit of growth but the flower is a clear, even sharp yellow, which does not seem to fade as the flowers mature. The edge of the corona is both widespread and frilled, and being a more positive color, it is a striking bulb when the pan is in full bloom.

Narcissus bulbocodium var. *mesatlanticus.* Deep yellow form. Award of Merit R.H.S.

N. *romieuxii.* Form #1. 10 Y-Y.

This is one of the main allies of *N. bulbocodium* growing in North Africa, the other being *N. romieuxii* subsp. *albidus.* The basic form—and I use that term loosely—is a bulb, typically *bulbocodium,* which grows in much the same manner as *N. cantabricus.* Foliage is usually quite fine, although not stiff and tuft-like as with some of the *N. bulbocodiums* var. *conspicuus* forms. Growth in pans starts early so budding can usually be seen in late November. Buds develop briskly and the pan is usually in full bloom the week before Christmas. Flowering continues well into January. The flower stems are 4–6 in. (10–15 cm) tall and the flowers have a fairly wide-flaring corona and a pale sulphur-yellow color. The flowers open a clear yellow and fade slightly as they mature. The perianth tube is narrow, usually a pale green, but clearly lacks the bell shaped curve of *N. cantabricus*. The bulbs grow without difficulty, do not seem subject to basal rot, and perform well.

I am growing a number of selected forms which have seemed to be sufficiently distinct as to warrant separation.

N. romieuxii. Form #2. 10 Y-Y.

These bulbs came to me from John Blanchard. The flowers differ from the usual in that the edge of the corona is deeply frilled, even crenulated. The degree of frilling seems to vary from year to year, but even when not so obvious is still of interest and value. Some seasons the flowers are so deeply frilled as to almost give the impression of being semi-double. The color is the same as form #1, a clear medium yellow. It grows just as freely as the type and without problems. A good bulb.

N. romieuxii. Form #3. 10 Y-Y.

This form came to me under the label "romieuxii good form" which is exactly what it is. Here appears to to be a fine example of the value of careful selection by a grower, who noted that one bulb was superior, segregated it and grew it on as a clone. The first time it bloomed for me I made the following notes: "Clear pale yellow which does not fade. Wide open, shallow but frilled cup. Looks good." This first assessment has been sustained in following seasons, so I have no hesitation in suggesting this as a superior selection from the basic type. The stems are slightly taller, 6–7 in. (15–17 cm), the flowers slightly larger, ½ in. (12–15 mm) wide and the general appearance good. Buds appear in early December and it is usually in full bloom by the end of that month.

The bulbs we have so far considered are all similar and of a color which could be classed as a light yellow. But there are as the reader might imagine, selections with deeper yellow flowers.

Narcissus romieuxii. Frilled form.

Plate 2. 1, *Narcissus romieuxii* subsp. *albidus* var. *zaianicus*; 2, *N. romieuxii*; 3, *N. bulbocodium* subsp. *pallidus* var. *praecox*; 4, *N. bulbocodium* subsp. *bulbocodium* var. *nivalis*; 5, *N. romieuxii* subsp. *albidus* var. *tananicus*; 6, *N. romieuxii* subsp. *albidus* var. *kesticus*; 7, *N. romieuxii* var. *mesatlanticus*; 8, *N. cantabricus* subsp. *monophyllus*; 9, *N. bulbocodium* subsp. *bulbocodium* var. *genuinus*.

N. romieuxii. Yellow Form #1. 10 Y-Y.

This came to me under its collection number, JCA 805Y, as originally collected by Jim Archibald in Morocco. It is different in that the habit of growth is more dwarf, the foliage more dense and tufted, although the leaves individually are quite thin and semi-prostrate. The stem is short, 3–4 in. (8–10 cm) at most and the corona of the flower is spread wide, almost but not quite equal to *N. cantabricus* subsp. *petunioides.* I have called the color medium yellow, but this depends to some degree upon the age of the blooms.

The bulbs grow well without trouble, are amazingly floriferous, sending up three, four, and up to five blooms from a good bulb. My notes have consistently classed this as "very good" which I believe it to be. These bulbs are, I am sure, not a clone, for when the pan is in full bloom, very small differences can be noted between some of the flowers.

N. romieuxii. Yellow Form #2. 'Julia Jane'. 10 Y-Y.

When collecting the bulbs under the number 805Y (Yellow Form #1) Jim Archibald noted one particular bulb which seemed to be larger in every way from the basic swarm. This was kept separate and grown on as an individual bulb. This bulb, therefore, is a clone. It is an excellent example of a plantsman taking note of an outstanding specimen, a procedure which almost every grower practices, sometimes without realizing it.

And what a good selection this bulb was! One can best describe it as a clear yellow *petunioides* for the flowers are as large and as wide spread when fully mature

Narcissus romieuxii. Yellow form #2. Although a selection from the wild this has been named 'Julia Jane'.

as the best *petunioides.* There is only one small difference which can detract from this bulb when in flower. The texture and substance of the flat corona is not quite as solid as *petuniodes,* so that when the flower is fully open the flat corona may wilt slightly during the heat of the day in the greenhouse. The answer is to keep them cool and to grow them as hard as possible so this minor fault will not be apparent.

When it was eventually released by Jim Archibald, it carried the name of 'Julia Jane' and it is under this label that the bulb has been grown. It is a very good selection from the wild, vegetatively propagated as a clone. It grows just as well as the rest, gives no trouble, and is a pleasure when in bloom. Here, surely, is a bulb which might be used to make some interesting crosses.

N. romieuxii. White Form. JCA 805 W. 10 W-W.

Collected at the same time and from the same group as 805Y by Jim Archibald, it is almost exactly the same as #805Y excepting in the color of the flowers. These open a pale cream which slowly fades as the flowers mature until they are almost— but not quite white. But it is much closer to a true white than the standard yellow forms with which we began. The bulb is a good grower, flowers profusely— qualities for which I am continually looking.

N. romieuxii var. rifanus. 10 Y-Y.

This plant seems so similar to *mesatlanticus* that I have wondered why it was given a specific name, presumably indicating it was collected from the Rif Mountains. It is also the only variety in this group that has given me any trouble with basal rot. There seems to be no obvious advantage in this over other forms.

N. bulbocodium subsp. vulgaris. 10 Y-Y.

This name—*vulgaris*—used to be applied as the subspecies name which included such bulbs as *conspicuus, nivalis* and others. Gray so lists them in his 1961 catalog. However, the subspecies name of *vulgaris* seems to have been dropped in some instances and not in others. The form *genuinus* is sometimes listed as *vulgaris* forma *genuinus* and sometimes simply as *genuinus.* Two forms with the prefix *vulgaris* have recently come to hand—*N. bulbocodium* subsp. *vulgaris* var. *pallidus*

Narcissus bulbocodium var. *praecox.*
A most excellent and sturdy bulb.

Narcissus bulbocodium var. *pallidus.* Equally strong and sturdy.

and *N. bulbocodium* subsp. *vulgaris* var. *praecox,* both from Michael Salmon. In his latest review he omits the name *vulgaris* and lists them simply as forms of *bulbocodium.*

They are both excellent, found, according to Salmon, from Casablanca through the Zaian Mountains and east through the foothills of the Middle Atlas. They are particularly noteworthy for their sturdy, vigorous habit; stiff solid stems from 7–9 in. (18–23 cm) high, surmounted by quite large flowers with a wide, bell-shaped corona. Both range in color from a pale yellow to a strong canary-yellow. *N. bulbocodium* var. *praecox* is the first to flower, usually in full bloom by mid-January, while *N. bulbocodium* var. *pallidus* flowers about a month later. The flowers on both can be so large as to challenge in size the *N. bulbocodium* var. *citrinus* 'Landes,' considered to be one of the largest forms when it was first collected in the south of France. Both these bulbs perform essentially the same purpose as *N. bulbocodium* var. *conspicuus* with which we commenced this group, but they flower in January and February with *conspicuus* following in March.

N. romieuxii subsp. *albidus.* 10 Y-Y.

Michael Salmon, in his recent review of North African narcissus, does not use *bulbocodium* as part of the name, although it is clearly a member of the Section Bulbocodium. In much the same way that *N. cantabricus* has been reduced to a single name, so is this called *albidus* by some.

Narcissus romieuxii subsp. *albidus.*

I grow a number of individual plants [collected under number] with some better than others. Although the name might suggest that the flowers are white, this is not strictly accurate, for although some are white, there are many graduations leaning towards light yellow, depending upon both the bulb and the age of the flowers.

The first bulb I received under this name took two years to bloom. But when it did, what a beauty! The foliage is rather sparse, even insignificant, which can lead one to suppose that the bulb is a poor grower. But not so, it is just a quiet type that does nothing to suggest the quality and grace of the flower, when it finally appears. From the center of the two or three leaves a bud appears in early December, but development is slow so it will not mature until mid-January. The developed flower is quite large with a fairly broad but elongated corona on top of a 3–4 in. (8–10 cm) stem. The corona, held at right angles to the stem, is almost a trumpet, and the color can best be described as an off-white, or white with a pale yellow tinge. There is a distinct green stripe down the outside. I realize as I write that this does not sound particularly outstanding, yet this flower has that indefinable something, call it grace if you will, which in my opinion sets it apart. It does have one serious fault and that is that it is slow to increase. In four years my original bulb has become three, and this year I had three good flowers. I have selfed the flowers and obtained seeds which germinated freely, so perhaps this is the way to go. However, it will be sometime before I achieve a full pan, which, when mature, should be outstanding.

Narcissus romieuxii subsp. *albidus*. A very good form collected in Morocco.

N. romieuxii subsp albidus. White Form. 10 W-W.

This form is pure white. I have been growing it for some time under the name *N. bulbocodium* var. *tananicus*, but Michael Salmon states quite clearly that this is incorrect. The bulb which we have been growing under this last name has a small flower with a very short perianth tube, and a small, bowl-shaped corona. It is crystalline white and the flowers are usually held upright on short 3–4 in. (8–10 cm) stems. This bulb, Salmon states, is not *tananicus*, but a form of *N. romieuxii* subsp. *albidus*. The color is good and it is an interesting little bulb, but of importance only to the collector.

N. romieuxii subsp. albidus var. tananicus. 10 Y-Y.

I received bulbs of this variety a year ago, collected by Michael Salmon in Morocco. It has just flowered for the first time. Fairly large funnel-shaped flowers are held at a strict right angle to the stem. In color it is a deeper yellow than most of the *albidus* forms, yet it seems to vary and I have bulbs which are nearly white. In many of the more recent collections of this group, still under number, some have bloomed with clear white flowers quite up to the clear, sharp form of many of the *cantabricus*. The only difference between the *albidus* forms and the *cantabricus* forms is the bell-shape of the perianth tube as described by Michael Salmon. I am sure that before long we shall receive further collected additions to the *albidus* group which will greatly enhance the range and quality of plants available.

Narcissus romieuxii subsp. *albidus* var. *zaianicus* forma lutescens.

N. romieuxii subsp. *albidus* var. *zaianicus* forma. *lutescens.* 10 Y-Y.

What a name to give to any small bulb! To the botanist or latin scholar it means something, but to the horticulturist it indicates a more or less white form of *albidus,* collected in the Zaian mountains. It is an excellent bulb, having all the easy habits of most of the North African species, and flowers profusely. It also has the advantage of being generally available. It develops much earlier than any of the others, budding in October, and is usually in full flower by the end of November. The stem is taller than some, 6–8 in. (15–20 cm) and the flowers are a fairly large, wide, open cup. It is supposed to be white, but mine changes from year to year. At times they appear almost completely white, and in other years closer to a pale yellow. It is a pleasing flower, particularly en-masse, and it seems to settle down and produce this effect regularly after two or three years. "Lutescens" I am told means "becoming yellow" and I have recently received bulbs called simply *N. romieuxii* subsp. *albidus* var. *zaianicus.* These have not yet flowered but it is possible that they may prove to be a pure white.

Bulbocodium Hybrids

There are very few cultivars derived from the Bulbocodium division. It appears that the bulbocodiums have not appealed to hybridizers, who as a group seem to prefer larger and brighter flowers of the more typical forms which flower at "narcissus time." The bulbocodiums do not conform to these rigid limitations, and although they cross freely with each other and most other *Narcissus* species, the number of named cultivars is remarkably small.

'Elfhorn'. Alec Gray. 1948. 12 Y-Y. Camborne, Cornwall, England.

Registered by Alec Gray in 1948, yet he does not mention it in his book nor is it listed in his 1961 catalog. I obtained bulbs from New Zealand but in four years they have yet to flower. Unless it is quite exceptional when it does bloom, this cultivar is likely to be discarded. Parentage unknown.

'Kenellis'. Gray 1948. *N. bulbocodium* var. *citrinus* × 'Snowflake'. 12 W-Y.

One of Alec Gray's early hybrids. The flowers are more of the trumpet type, slightly drooping, and opening a pale yellow fading to white. Although this is classified as a miniature, it could be argued that it ought to be an intermediate, if there was such a category. Rather too large for pan culture, I have moved mine to the garden where it grows quite well. If grown in a pan it comes into bloom in early March.

'Kenellis'. One of Alec Gray's early hybrids.

The Blanchard Group of Hybrids. D. Blanchard. Blandford. Dorset, England.

A number of crosses were made by Douglas Blanchard using good forms of *N. cantabricus* and *N. romieuxii* which I have chosen to keep together as a group, because they were some of the first hybrids made using forms of *bulbocodium*. They are also known as the "fabric group" because some are named after different forms of cloth. As a group all are of typical *bulbocodium* form, with thin, grass-like foliage, stiff stems 6–8 in. (15–20 cm) high and flowers of varying shapes and sizes, opening cream and fading to a crisp white. All seem to have acquired a fair degree of "hybrid vigor" and thus grow very well, flower profusely, and when grown rather lean in a pan the result can be quite spectacular. I can heartily recommend them all as superior plants for pan culture where bloom is wanted from November onwards. Most are also readily available.

'Jessamy', Blanchard 1952. 12 W-W. *N. romieuxii* × *N. cantabricus* var. *foliosus.*

Opens in mid-November with a chalice-shaped cup of pale yellow, which slowly fades through cream to an off-white. The bulb grows strongly and increases rapidly.

'Nylon', Blanchard 1949. *N. romieuxii* × *N. cantabricus* subsp. *monophyllus.* 12 W-W.

This cultivar came into commerce as a group so that bulbs grown under this name from different sources vary slightly. I have collected 5 slightly different forms and have selected one which I think the best. It is now being propagated as a clone. It has the typical cream to off-white flowers, with the edge of the corona slightly frilled. It is one of the most prolific flowering bulbs in the group, each bulb producing from two to four good flowers. A pan full of bulbs appears as a tumbling sheet of flowers.

'Nylon'. One of the first series of Blanchard hybrids.

'Taffeta'. A later Blanchard hybrid.

'Taffeta'. Blanchard 1952. 12 W-W. *N. cantabricus* **var.** *foliosus* × *N. romieuxii.*

Another of the "fabric group" which flowers early in November. It has quite large white flowers, with a broad, open corona. It is very similar to 'Tarlatan' in many ways but not quite so large.

'Tarlatan', Blanchard 1952. 12 W-W. *N. cantabricus* **var.** *foliosus* × *N. romieuxii.*

This cultivar probably has the largest flowers of the group. Blooming in mid-November, it produces many large white flowers with a wide open corona, opening a pale cream which fades to white as the flowers mature.

Two other names which may crop up in this "Fabric" group are 'Poplin' and 'Muslin.' I have flowered 'Poplin,' but it seems to have no point of value over those already listed. I have not seen 'Muslin' and doubt that it is now grown.

'Tiffany'. Blanchard 1960. 12 W-W.

I understand this is an F2 hybrid.

An excellent bulb, superficially the same as some of the others but which flowers about a month later. The flowers are larger than 'Jessamy' with a more widely flared corona. Opening a pale yellow and fading to white, this is one of the last of this group to flower, and thus provides an excellent succession.

'Trimon'. A natural hybrid between *N. triandrus* and *N. cantabricus*.

'Trimon'. A. W. Tait 1899. 12 W-W. Collected in Portugal.

This is listed as a wild hybrid between *N. triandus albus* and probably *N. cantabricus* subsp. *monophyllus*—hence the name. My bulbs came from John Blanchard, who states that they were collected in the wild comparatively recently so this can hardly be the original form. Be that as it may, there is an excellent illustration of 'Trimon' in Calvert's *Daffodil Growing for Pleasure and Profit,* and the plant I have is exactly the same as illustrated.

It is a gem. The leaves are not so profuse and dense as other bulbocodiums and the stems tend to be rather short, 3–4 in. (8–10 cm). The flowers appear much later, from early February onwards; are quite large with a wide open cup; and of a crisp yet slightly creamy white. It is difficult to put into words but this little bulb is another, similar to *N. triandrus* subsp. *pallidulus* var. *aurantiacus,* which simply possesses an air of grace and substance that, in my opinion, sets it right apart. Last year my pan began to bud in mid-December, was showing color in mid-January and was in full bloom on February 20. It increases rather slowly, but grows without difficulty, and once a full pan has been achieved it is a delight.

I have been advised that the name 'Trimon' is no longer acceptable and that the plant should now be called *N. munozii-germandei!!* The exclamation marks are mine. Whatever, a bulb which looks remarkably like the 'Trimon' of 1899 is growing in my greenhouse and moreover it received an Award of Merit from the R.H.S. in February, 1899. I look for its coming each year with impatience and always regret its passing.

As far as I know this brings us to the end of the known *bulbocodium* hybrids. It will immediately be apparent that there is plenty of room here for more hybridizing. I have heard of some work being done in this direction in California, but have not yet seen any results. I have been working on such a project in a modest way, crossing a good form of *N. triandrus* with *N. cantabricus* subsp. *petunioides*. A number of these crosses have flowered and look quite interesting. The flowers are fairly large, usually produced in two's and sometimes three's on rather short 4 in. (10 cm) stems. They range in color from deep cream to a brilliant crisp white. They all come into bloom in mid-February indoors, and almost without exception have the rather thick, glaucus and twisted prostrate foliage typical of *N. triandrus*. But perhaps more interesting is the fact that most of the bulbs are substantially larger than either parent which might suggest that they may possess a degree of hybrid vigor which would allow them to be grown and enjoyed in the garden rather than in pans. Time will tell.

CHAPTER SEVEN

The Trumpet Daffodils

DIVISIONS 1 and 2

This Section, now known as Pseudonarcissus (previously Ajax) contains a number of important species, both standard and miniature, which have been largely responsible for the many hybrids we typically think of as daffodils. Those which are quite large in both height and flower do not have a place here, and the number of species which do conform to the limitations of a true miniature are strictly limited.

N. asturiensis. 10 Y-Y

This is one of the best-known species, formerly named most appropriately *N. minimus*. A complete and accurate miniature replica of the traditional trumpet daffodil is produced on 3–4 in. (7.5–10 cm) stems, but the flower is so small that one can only marvel at its perfection. The bright yellow corona is about ¾ in. (20 mm) long and about ½ in. (12 mm) wide, with the perianth segments (petals) proportioned to match. The species is however extremely variable, so these dimensions approximate the average run of material, usually offered as collected bulbs. The quantities available on the mountains of Spain seem inexhaustible, and demand has until now been filled by annual collections. This however, is likely to cease before long, because it is no longer possible to import such material into the United States.

The bulb itself is quite small with a light brown tunic, which starts into growth very early in the season. In pans, leaves appear in late November. Just as the tips are barely visible, the top of the flower bud can often be seen thrusting up from the center. Bulbs are usually not long-lived in cultivation, lasting perhaps two or three seasons. Practically none increase by division, so stock is best replenished by regular sowing of seed from flowers which have been selfed. The flowers themselves are a delightful and exquisitely chiseled model of a large trumpet daffodil, with a proportionate but long corona, frequently with heavily frilled edges. The flowers are a clear medium yellow and begin opening soon after Christmas in pans.

Unfortunately, the material available has two faults. First, being collected, the bulbs are not clonal and do not flower at the same time, flowering being intermittent and spotty over a two month period. Secondly, most flowers are born on rather weak stems, so that they droop on the ground. I have recently received newer collections which have a much better stem, but it is clear that a wide-open opportunity exists for the selection of a bulb which is longer-lived, will increase by

Narcissus asturiensis.

Narcissus asturiensis 'Giant'.

Comparison between normal and giant form of *Narcissus asturiensis.*

division, and which has a stiffer stem.

With these qualities in mind I also have another form which came to me as *N. asturiensis* 'Giant' which is exactly what it is. Reputedly collected in Spain by Frank Waley, this is a much stronger and larger bulb, with stems from 8–10 in. (20–25 cm) high and a flower size to match. It is odd to see both forms in flower side by side for the larger form is so exact a replica of the basic form, but about four times as large, complete with long corona and a deeply serrated edge. This is clearly a clone, for the bulbs grow evenly and flower together. However it does not have the daintiness of the true species.

In a recent meeting with Michael Salmon, I learned that two additional forms have recently been collected from Northern Spain which tend to fill the gap between *N. asturiensis* and others in the pseudonarcissus section of a standard size. They are *N. jacetanus* and *N. jacetanus,* var. *vasconicus*. I now have two bulbs of each, and beyond the fact that they come from a limestone area, I know nothing about them. *N. jacetanus* may well prove to be the form I have been growing as *N. asturiensis* 'Giant' but a rough sketch by Michael Salmon indicates that the var. *vasconicus* is quite unusual. The foliage is prostrate and the single flower on a short stem is shaped in a curious manner, so that the corona resembles a small vase. The frilled edge first narrows and then expands to a wider base where it joins the petals at the base of the flower. I shall watch with eager interest when these reach flowering size.

N. capax plenus see *N. eystettensis*

N. nanus see *N. minor*

N. minor. **10 Y-Y.**

This is the next step up in size from *N. asturiensis* and is the species which I believe is frequently photographed and shown as *N. asturiensis.* Both have the typical broad, strap-like leaves of the traditional daffodil. It was formerly called *N. nanus,* a name no longer valid. Gray also lists *N. nanus* as a synonym for *N. minor* var. *conspicuus,* so just where we stand I do not know.

However, there is a bulb freely available under the name *N. minor* which is a larger and sturdier version of *N. asturiensis.* The flowers are perhaps twice as large but similar in form and color, produced on 4–6 in. (10–15 cm) stems which are stiff and do not droop. It is a good bulb readily available from most suppliers.

N. minor **var. *conspicuus* see** *N. minor*

N. minor **var. *pumilus.* 10 Y-Y**

This is supposed to be a slightly larger form of *N. minor* but I have never been able to make a clear distinction. A good clump of *N. minor* is first class anyway.

N. minor **'pumilus plenus'. 4 Y-Y.**

This form, also known as N. 'Rip van Winkle,' seems to be a good grower, indoors or out in the garden. Stems are about 6 in. (15 cm) high with flowers in proportion. It is a complete double and can produce such a heavy head that the flowers are again prone to bow down into the mud. It is best enjoyed in the garden, but does require some support to keep the flowers erect. As a general rule I do not like double flowers, because they tend to be out of proportion and top heavy. This is true of *N. minor* 'Pumilus Plenus' so although I have it I do not suggest that it be at the top of anyone's buying list.

Narcissus minor pumilus plenus. Also known as N. Rip Van Winkle.

Narcissus moschatus var. *alpestris* A delight, but difficult to grow.

N. *moschatus* var. *alpestris.* 10 W-W.

This white sub-species in the Pseudonarcissus Section is outstanding. The basic form is *N. pseudonarcissus* subsp. *moschatus* which produces its delightful, milk-white trumpets on stems 10–12 in. (25–30 cm) high. The manner in which these flowers are held on the stem is also unique, for they crook right over, and hang vertically downwards like a cluster of long, white bells.

The miniature form, known as *N. pseudonarcissus* subsp. *moschatus* var. *alpestris* is similar in every way but does not grow more than 4–5 in. (10–12.5 cm) high. Hung on each stem is the white, drooping trumpet, smaller to be in proportion, surrounded by twisted petals of the same color. It is a delight to see in bloom but very difficult to grow.

I started off some years ago with five modest bulbs, and one by one they faded away until I was down to one, which seemed to be more robust than the others. This tough one has now developed into three and so I am slowly creeping up again. With problems such as this, one must never give up. This first lot was also difficult in other ways; it could not be selfed to produce seed, nor would it cross with any other bulb. This bulb clearly had a rather limited value. A year or so later I received three more bulbs, which, when they flowered, appeared identical to the first. However, the three continued to prosper, and the flowers proved to be fertile both as pollen and seed parents. This second collection is therefore much more likely to succeed than the first.

Unfortunately the ordinary *N. pseudonarcissus* subsp. *moschatus* is frequently offered under the name of *alpestris*. *N. moschatus* grows more easily so one can be deluded into thinking that one has acquired a fine form which has enabled one to succeed where others have failed. The true *alpestris* is clearly a most difficult bulb to grow being highly susceptible to basal rot. But anyone having the true, really dwarf *N. pseudonarcissus* subsp. *moschatus* var. *alpestris,* and growing it well, can be considered an expert!

There are, of course, a number of species included in this Section Pseudonarcissus, some of which Alec Gray described in his book, species such as *N. obvallaris* and *N. pallidiflorus*. These I have omitted because they are not now classed as true miniatures.

N. nanus. **see *N. Minor.***

Pseudonarcissus Hybrids

The number of hybrids that have been developed in this group is quite large, and more are coming forward every year. I do not profess to have grown them all, but even if I cannot speak of every one first hand, I include them here.

'Bagatelle' Gerritsen and Son Holland 1965 I Y-Y

Bred by the Dutch company also responsible for most of the new split-corona cultivars. This cultivar is very similar to 'Little Gem,' *N. minor* and 'Wee Bee' but a good grower. Because it has stems about 9 in. (23 cm) high I prefer to grow it outside.

'Bambi.' G. Zandbergen-Terwegen. Holland. 1948. I W-Y.

Alec Gray included this cultivar in his book, and I do also, although it is not on the Approved List of Miniatures. It is a first-class bulb and readily available at a moderate price. One of the first to flower in the cool-house, it is usually in full bloom by Christmas, and by early March outside. The stems are 6–8 in. (15–20 cm) tall and the flowers are held stiffly erect. Although common, it is a good bulb and a bicolor with white petals and yellow corona.

'Bowle's Bounty'. E. A. Bowles. Enfield, England. 1948. 1 Y-Y.

Although this hybrid has been around for 30 years I have not yet grown it. Very early, it was described as a soft sulphur trumpet produced on stems 6–8 in. (15–20 cm) tall. E. A. Bowles was an extremely skilled horticulturist who was responsible for introducing many plants, all of them clearly superior. This daffodil, therefore, comes from the right place and with an excellent reputation. It should be a good bulb.

'Candlepower'. Alec Gray. Camborne, England. 1975. 1 W-W.

Only recently have I been able to obtain and grow this cultivar, for it is highly regarded and much sought after. Now that it is in bloom one can see that it really is a very good bulb. Quite small, with leaves not more than 3 in. (7.5 cm) long, the flower stem slightly surmounts them, and produces a most beautifully formed white trumpet, with a fairly long corona and a frilled edge. Although I have no information as to its parentage, there is no doubt that it has to be related to *N. asturiensis* because it flowers early, usually in full bloom on Valentine's Day. In this first season there have been no indications of cultural or disease problems. It is a most elegant little bulb which I am delighted to have.

'Bambi'. Easy, available, and inexpensive.

'Candlepower'. One of Alec Gray's best hybrids.

Plate 3. 1, *Narcissus pseudonarcissus* subsp. *pallidiflorus*; 2, *N. pseudonarcissus* subsp. *nobilis*; 3, *N. hispanicus*; 4, *N. pseudonarcissus* subsp. *moschatus* var. *alpestris*; 5, *N. pseudonarcissus* subsp. *obvallaris*; 6, *N. asturiensis*; 7, *N. pseudonarcissus* subsp. *nevadensis*.

'Charles Warren'. Alec Gray. Camborne, England. 1948. 1 Y-Y.

Although not included in his book, Alec Gray describes this cultivar in his 1961 catalog. He notes that it was found growing in a hedge in Cornwall. A true dwarf, the stems are not more than 5 in. (12.5 cm) tall, and the yellow trumpet is similar to but better than 'Wee Bee.' It also flowers earlier—mid-February in a pan. I have bulbs from two sources and although superficially the same the quality of the blooms on one is superior. This is a good bulb.

N. eystettensis 'Queen Anne's Double Daffodil.' 4 Y-Y.

This has been in cultivation for a very long time, and as far as is known, has never been found growing wild. It has been suggested that it is a natural hybrid between a dwarf form of _N. minor_ and _N. triandrus_. It is, therefore, classed as a hybrid, yet it bears no resemblance to _N. triandrus_ and appears to be a simple, double form, of a small, yellow trumpet. Gray lists it under another old name, _N. capax plenus_.

I can understand why this plant has not become more popular. Without exception, bulbs I have received have been poor and in most cases diseased. Clearly it is difficult to find clean bulbs, but if you obtain some, then you may have to attend closely for two or three years to clean them up.

When growing properly, the flower is more pleasing than 'Rip van Winkle' in that the stem is stronger, 6 in. (15 cm) or so in height, with bright yellow double flowers which appear as many-rayed yellow stars. It is a pleasant plant, particularly outside in the garden.

'Gambas'. Alec Gray. Camborne, England. 1964. I Y-Y

This is presumed to be a _N. asturiensis_ cross, but the parentage is uncertain. Although this is listed as 4 in. (10 cm) by Broadleigh Gardens in England, from whom I obtained my bulbs, it has produced its medium-sized, yellow trumpets on 6–8 in. (15–20 cm) stems here and has accordingly been planted out in the garden. It grows without difficulty, but is too large for pan culture and, as a yellow trumpet, becomes just one of a group from which it does not stand out in any way.

'Gipsy Queen'. Alec Gray. Camborne, England. 1969. 1 Y-WWY, _N. minor_ × _N. asturiensis_.

This is believed to be a cross between a white selection from _N. minor_—possibly 'Rockery White'—and _N. asturiensis_. I obtained this bulb in 1986 for the first time and it performs in exactly the same manner as 'Candlepower,' but of the two I would prefer the latter. It is too soon to say that 'Candlepower' is clearly the better form, especially as the two came from different suppliers. Both are superficially similar but at the moment I prefer 'Candlepower.' The height is the same, 3 in. (7.5 cm).

In connection with these two cultivars, both originating from Alec Gray as miniature white trumpets, I have heard recently of two other bulbs, presumably from the same cross, which are now being grown, one in North America and one in Ireland. I have seen the North American bulb and it looks very good indeed, so I have hopes that in the not too distant future we shall have a group of perhaps three or four cultivars, all originating from Alex Gray, which will fill the need for a truly small white trumpet.

'Kehelland'. Alec Gray. Camborne, England. 1946. 4 Y-Y

Presumably a double-flowered selection from _N. minor_, the parentage of this bulb is unknown. I have had little success with any of the double-flowered forms of narcissus. This bulb is a fairly robust grower, producing plenty of foliage and flower stems 7–8 in. (17–20 cm) tall, but when the buds start to develop the flower aborts and drys up. I have been told that this is due to growing at too high a temperature, but both in pans and in the garden results have been the same. Gray speaks well of this bulb but it has been a disappointment for me.

'Lilliput'. J. Gerritsen & Son. Holland. 1965. I W-Y.

This is in effect a refined 'Little Beauty' coming from the same Dutch breeder. No parentage is given. The flowers are a typical large, trumpet type, produced in mid-February indoors on stiff 5–6 in. (12.5–15 cm) stems. It is described as a 1 W-Y indicating that the flower has white petals and a yellow corona. This is not exactly true, for when the flowers mature, the deeply frilled and reflexed edge of the corona is a clear deep yellow, which slowly becomes paler until the base of the corona is practically white where it joins the truly white petals. A clearly superior bulb.

'Lilliput'. Not really small but a beauty.

'Little Beauty'. J. Gerritsen & Son. Holland. 1965. 1 W-Y.

This completes the trio of bulbs, superficially alike, all bicolors and originating in Holland. The first was 'Bambi' which has its place, is widely grown and generally available. Next in refinement comes this cultivar, while 'Lilliput' competes, and in my opinion, tops the group. But 'Little Beauty' is good, too. Quite small, from 4–6 in. (10–15 cm), the flowers are in proportion forming a bright yellow trumpet with white petals. It is, in effect, a superior 'Bambi.'

It is excellent for growing in pans or outside, and will be in flower in the coolhouse by mid-February. It is readily available at a modest price.

'Little Beauty'. Readily available at a modest cost.

'Little Gem'. J. Gerritsen & Son. Holland. 1959. 1 Y-Y.

I assume this to be a selection from *N. minor* for the differences between the two are minute. Either can be grown as a satisfactory and inexpensive, medium-sized, yellow trumpet.

'Marionette'. Alec Gray Camborne, England. 1946. 2 Y-YYR *N. asturiensis* × *N. poeticus*

Gray lists this as a 4 in. (10 cm) stem, and Havens, from where I obtained the bulb, as 5 in. (12.5 cm). In my pans it grew closer to 8 in. (20 cm) and, therefore, I planted it out where it has grown very well indeed, forming a fine, solid clump. The bright yellow flowers have a distinct orange-red rim on the corona, and are placed in Division II, the cup being smaller. An excellent bulb for the miniature border.

'Mustard Seed'. Alec Gray. Camborne, England. 1937. 2 Y-Y. *N. asturiensis* × *N. poeticus.*

One of Alec Gray's early hybrids which is a real miniature. The stems are not

'Little Gem'. Inexpensive and excellent in pans.

more than 2–3 in. (4–7 cm) and the flowers are small and dainty to match. Bright yellow, the corona is a deeper color still and also quite small—hence Division II. It grows without any problems and is ideal for pan culture.

'Rockery Beauty'. W. J. Eldering & Son. Holland. 1928. 1 W-Y.
'Rockery Gem'. R. Van der Schoot & Son. Holland. 1939. 1 W-W.
'Rockery White'. G. Zanbergen-Terwegan. Holland. 1936. 1 W-W.

I have not grown any of these so cannot speak from first hand experience. I am informed that 'Rockery White' is very difficult to bring into flower and none of them have qualities which might be an improvement on any now grown.

'Rosaline Murphy'. Alec Gray. Camborne, England. 1958. 2 Y-Y. *N. watieri* × *N. asturiensis.*

This is a real beauty for pan culture. A true miniature, the flowers, which are a pale cream, appear on top of 4–5 in. (10–12.5 cm) stems. The corona is slightly smaller than *N. asturiensis*, which places the bulb in Division II. The stems are erect and the flowers appear somewhat later than many, the pan usually being in full bloom by the second week in March. I have had a little trouble growing this bulb, or more correctly, storing the dry bulbs after they have died down. Two bulbs obtained in 1982 had increased to 26 in four growing seasons, but each summer I found two or three bulbs dry and useless when it came time to replant. This year they were planted with the special treatment reserved for the most touchy types, and results seem to be much better. Despite this modest problem, the pan is always a real pleasure and it remains one of my favorites.

'Rosaline Murphy'.

'Skelmersdale Gold'. Broadleigh Gardens, England. 1975. 1 Y-Y.
 I obtained bulbs of this from England, and when they bloomed they appeared to be yet another selection from *N. minor*. A plain, yellow trumpet on 6 in. (15 cm) stems, this cultivar did not do well for me, quickly dying presumably from basal rot. I think that there are a number of other bulbs very similar, and far easier to grow.

'Small Talk'. Grant Mitch. Oregon. 1965. 1 Y-Y.
 An open pollinated seedling of 'Wee Bee.' This is an excellent bulb. It grows very well in pans, where in the cool-house the bulbs are in full flower by mid-February. The flowers are quite similar to *N. minor* but slightly taller—8–9 in. (20–22.5 cm) of a deep chrome yellow with stiff stems. I class this as a refined and superior form of *N. minor*. The pan last year was rated "Very Good" and I have had no trouble with this bulb in any way.

'Small Talk'. A delight in a pan.

'Snug'. Alec Gray. Camborne, England. 1957. 1 W-W. Seedling of *N. alpestris*.

Gray describes this as a seedling with a much better constitution than its parent, and flowers about 5 in. (12.7 cm) tall. I am not at all sure that I have the correct bulb, for the one that I have under this name has grown well for three years but without flowering. I shall persist because it is a white form, which are few and far between, but hope my bulbs will flower soon. So it has one more year and then it's out, for there is no value in any bulb which does not perform. It may well be that 'Candlepower'is better anyway.

'Tanagra'. Alec Gray. Camborne, England. 1946. 1 Y-Y. *N. asturiensis* × *N. pseudo-narcissus* var. *obvallaris*.

Gray lists this as an early flowering bulb, with stems 5–6 in. (12–15 cm) high. I have only just obtained this and have yet to see it flower. Looking at the foliage I have the impression that it is rather an ordinary bulb. I could be wrong, but a number of Gray's very early hybrids have been superseded by newer and better forms.

'Tiny Tot'. Matthew Fowlds. USA. 1975. 1 Y-Y. *N. cyclamineus* × *N. asturiensis*.

This cross was made first, and then two seedlings which resulted were again crossed to produce 'Tiny Tot.' Strangely, there is no obvious sign of *N. cyclamineus*, for the flowers appear to be a slightly larger and more refined form of *N. asturiensis*, falling somewhere between it and *N. minor*. The stems are about 5 in. (12.5 cm) high

'Tiny Tot'.

and the flowers are sufficiently close to the larger trumpet forms to allow this to be placed in Division I. It is an excellent bulb with no faults as far as I can determine. This cultivar could be grown as a good replacement for *N. asturiensis,* for the effect is the same but without any of the limitations and disadvantages of the species. Three bulbs have become 11 in three growing seasons. It is splendid for pan culture, and is in full bloom by mid-February.

'Tosca'. Alec Gray. Camborne, England. 1969. 1 W-Y. *N. asturiensis* × 'Little Beauty'.
    The flower on this cultivar is different, for the petals are pearl-white with the cup lemon-yellow. It is listed as being not more than 4 in. (10 cm) but for me it grew much taller, 7–8 in. (17–20 cm) and so I planted it outside where it does very well. Not really suitable for pan culture but excellent outside.

'Tweeny'. Alec Gray. Camborne, England. 1950. 2 W-Y.
    Gray states that this was bred from a large Division II seedling and *N. watieri.* It flowers very late with flowers on a 6 in. (15 cm) stem. White petals and a citron-yellow cup. A number of growers seem to want this form, but all the bulbs I have purchased until recently have been riddled with stripe and so performed badly. This year I obtained three more. One was clearly striped, so was grubbed out and discarded. The other two look fine, but one bulb has dark green foliage while the other is clearly glaucus. They are similar in size but clearly not the same. I mention this as being the usual state of affairs when one is trying to obtain a bulb. And even now I am not at all certain that this cultivar is worth the effort.

Comparison of 'Wee Bee' and 'Small Talk'. 'Wee Bee' smallest. 'Small Talk' largest.

'Wee Bee'. Zanbergen-Terwegan. Holland. 1948. 1 Y-Y.

This cultivar is a selection from *N. minor*. It is a good form having all the qualities of *N. minor,* but with a slightly improved flower on a 5 in. (12.5 cm) stem.

In this area we do have a close group of small yellow trumpets which are so similar as to suggest that a modest weeding out would be helpful. *N. minor,* 'Charles Warren,' 'Gambas,' 'Little Gem,' 'Small Talk,' and 'Wee Bee' are all very close. Although generally available, 'Wee Bee' would not be my first choice.

'W. P. Milner'. William Backhouse. England. 1884. 2 Y-Y.

As can be seen, this cultivar is just over 100 years old, and its inherent qualities must be sound for it is still grown and enjoyed. *N. pseudonarcissus* subsp. *moschatus* var. *alpestris* or perhaps *N. pseudonarcissus* subsp. *moschatus* itself must be in its heritage somewhere, because it is very similar to both, with the stems up to 10 in. (25 cm) in height, upon which are born creamy white, drooping flowers. I grow mine outdoors in the miniature border, for it seems somewhat tall for good pan culture.

'W. P. Milner'. An old but delightful cultivar.

This brings us to the end of the list of miniature trumpet daffodils. I have omitted some, because although they are on the Approved List of Miniatures, I have not grown them and in most instances they are difficult to obtain. These include the following:

'Minidaf'. J. Gerritsen & Son. Holland. 1970. 1 Y-Y
'Morwenna'.R. R. Backhouse.England.1938.2 Y-Y
'Petit Beurre'.J. Gerritsen & Son. Holland.1971.1 Y-Y
'Picarillo'. B. O. Mulligan.Washington.1951.2 Y-Y
'Piccolo'.J. Gerritsen & Son.Holland.1967.1 Y-Y
'Pledge'.W. Jefferson-Brown.England.1978.1 W-W
'Rupert'.Alec Gray.Camborne, England.1961.1 W-Y
'Sir Echo'.J. N. Hancock.Australia.1968.2 Y-R
'Sneezy'.Alec Gray.Camborne, England.1956.1 Y-Y
'Sprite'.Alec Gray.Camborne, England.1972.1 W-W

But without these we still have a group which is excellent in every way and a delight to grow.

Plate 4. 1, *Narcissus triandrus* subsp. *pallidulus* var. *aurantiacus*; 2, *N. triandrus* subsp. *pallidulus*; 3, *N. poeticus* subsp. *poeticus*; 4, *N. triandrus* subsp. *trandrus*; 5, *N. tazetta* subsp. *tazetta*; 6, *N. tazetta* subsp. *polyanthus*; 7, *N. tazetta* subsp. *papyraceus*; 8, *N. hedraeanthus*.

CHAPTER EIGHT

Narcissus Triandrus

DIVISION 5

Division 5 is another area in which it is difficult to be botanically exact. At one time the species was divided into seven named forms, but this has now been reduced to three by *Flora Europaea*. Unfortunately, it will take at least 10 years for this information to filter down to growers and others offering bulbs. I shall, therefore, attempt to cross reference the names still in use.

N. triandrus subsp. *triandrus*.

Grouped under this heading are the forms which were previously known as *N. triandrus* var. *albus*, *N. triandrus* var. *cernuus* and *N. triandrus* var. *pulchellus* mostly originating from northern Spain and Portugal. *N. triandrus* var. *cernuus* was reputed to have pendent or hanging flowers—hence the name—but all *triandrus* have this habit. It was also supposed to be a bicolor, and in truth I have yet to see a really good bicolor in this species. Some may open with the corona a deeper color and the petals cream, but this difference quickly fades as the flowers mature.

N. triandrus var. *pulchellus* does offer some reason for being kept separate. The name indicates that it is presumed to be more beautiful than most, and again it is supposed to be more or less bicolor, with a creamy white cup and yellow petals. The form is certainly most attractive, producing fairly strong stems from 5–7 in. (12–17 cm) tall with from 1–5 flowers in which the corona or cup is smaller than some, being just about as long as it is wide, i.e. ⅜ in. (10 mm). This alters the overall balance of the flower, and produces a most charming effect, especially when a stem with two, three or more florets is produced.

Although the name *N. triandrus* var. *albus* is included here, I do not think this is a valid name, although it has been and no doubt will continue to be, loosely applied to the entire group. Bulbs are regularly offered as *N. triandrus* var. *albus,* when in fact they produce flowers of every type and color from pale cream to light yellow, none of which could rightly be considered white. An occasional bulb will appear with clear, pure white flowers, but due to the fact that stocks offered for sale are almost exclusively collected and therefore seedlings, the mixed effect will continue. Vegetative propagation of a truly white form is not usually satisfactory.

Most bulbs of triandrus seem to be relatively short-lived, so stocks are maintained either by collection from the wild or by sowing self-pollinated seed. In either case the result is the same, a mixed grill of shapes, sizes and colors typical of the plant in the wild. It has been virtually impossible to offer a true clone of any of the *triandrus* subspecies because collection is still too easy. But the time will come when

Narcissus triandrus subsp. *triandrus*.

the raping of the Spanish hills is no longer permitted and collecting is stopped. Then perhaps we shall have a true *N. triandrus* var. *albus* propagated either by division or perhaps tissue culture and/or twin scaling.

The leaves of most bulbs in this group tend to be glaucus, some having quite a distinct bluish tinge, and also to be prostrate rather than erect when mature. Some forms will produce three or four quite strong leaves which will curl and twist across the top of the pan in a most curious manner.

N. triandrus **var.** *albus* **see** *N. triandrus* **subsp.** *triandrus*

N. triandrus **var.** *aurantiacus* **see** *N. triandrus* **subsp.** *pallidulus*

N. triandrus **var.** *calathinus* **see** *N. triandrus* **subsp.** *capax*

N. triandrus **var.** *concolor* **see** *N. triandrus* **subsp.** *pallidulus*

N. triandrus **var.** *loiseleuri* **see** *N. triandrus* **subsp** *capax*

N. triandrus **subsp.** *pallidulus*.

This subspecies now includes bulbs previously listed as *N. triandrus* var. *aurantiacus* and *N. triandrus* var. *concolor*. In height and general form *N. triandrus* subsp. *N. triandrus* subsp. *pallidulus* is similar to the basic type, i.e. stem from 5–8 in. (12–20

Narcissus triandrus subsp. *pallidulus.*

cm) high and with 1–6 flowers per stem. The foliage on the typical form of *N. triandrus* subsp. *pallidulus* tends to be more or less erect and dark green in color. The flowers, which vary in size, also vary in color from pale cream to a clear primrose yellow. If fifty bulbs are acquired, many differences will be seen between individuals some being much stronger than others, with 3–5 flowers per stem. The corona will be of average length, ⅜–½ in. (10–13 mm), and usually with a distinct yellow cast, varying in intensity.

N. *triandrus* subsp. *pallidulus* var. *aurantiacus* once had its own identity but is now submerged into *pallidulus*. This edict I find most difficult to accept, for if ever a form is clearly different, this is it.

All the triandrus are a pleasure when in bloom, but *aurantiacus* has to be the gem. When the plant starts into growth one might be excused for expecting that it will turn out to be a form of *bulbocodium*. First leaves are quite fine, even thread-like, and give little indication of what is to come. Early in January small buds appear and a month later the first flowers open. The flower stem is rather more slender than other forms, and is usually not more than 4–6 in. (10–15 cm) tall. When the delicate, golden flowers appear, one or sometimes two on the end of a firm but slender stem, the grower knows it is a *triandrus*.

I use the term "gem" advisedly, for when in bloom one sees an exquisite, miniature, golden bell, delicately hung on the end of a fine wire, ready to tinkle in the breeze. Does this sound stupidly lyrical? I hope so for when this bulb is in flower I can hardly keep my eyes from it. It is a sheer delight.

Narcissus triandrus subsp. *pallidulus* var. *aurantiacus*. A perfect wild species for pan culture.

N. triandrus var. pulchellus see N. triandrus subsp. triandrus

N. triandrus subsp. capax.

This, the third subspecies to be recognized, has a long and quite interesting history. The bulb originates from the Isle Drenac, which is part of the Isles de Glenans group off the coast of France near Finisterre. How this bulb came to be there is a complete mystery for when taken from the island to the mainland it proved to be less hardy than most of the others. How then did it reach these islands and from where? J. G. Baker, in his review of the genus *Narcissus* published in 1875, accords it species status simply upon the length of its corona. He also says that similar forms have been found in Portugal, the truth of which is born out by current collectors, who note that forms closely resembling the Drenac bulb have been found in Portugal. Originally known as *N. calathinus,* the name was changed about 1908 to *N. triandrus* var. *loiseleurii* until it was noticed that it had previously been recorded as *capax.* Thus it now becomes *N. triandrus* subsp. *capax* and I hope that the botanists will leave their dusty archives alone so that this name can remain.

The bulb has been known since the early 1800's, and has been cultivated for nearly two centuries because of its quite outstanding qualities. The bulb is generally much more robust in all its parts than other types. The foliage is quite stout, appearing even slightly succulent, and dark green with a distinct gloss. As they develop, the tops tend to curl over upon themselves in a manner quite unique.

Narcissus triandrus subsp. *capax*. Difficult to find. Difficult to grow.

The stem is thick, and somewhat taller—6–9 in. (15–23 cm)—and the flowers are distinctly larger with the white corona nearly as long as the petals, i.e. from ¾ to 1 in. (20–25 mm). It is recorded that a pale sulphur yellow form has been seen. As there are no other forms of *triandrus* on the Isles of Glenans it can be assumed that this bulb has developed there as a clone, so propagation by self-pollinated seed seems the best way to keep it going.

It is reputed to be less hardy but I have not attempted to grow it outside and cannot comment. The inherent qualities of this sub species are so clear that it has been used almost exclusively as the form of *triandrus* in breeding the many revered *triandrus* hybrids which we now enjoy.

There is no doubt that a number of different bulbs are sold under this name, and it has taken me nearly seven years to obtain a bulb which I know to be true. During this time I have received four different bulbs, none of which were right.

One of these was a hybrid raised by Alec Gray and called 'Ivory Gate.' It produces bunches of large, creamy flowers of *triandrus* form and substantial size, but which lack the typical reflexed petals of the true species. It is easy to be deluded into believing that this is the exceptional plant from Brittany, but not so. It also lacks the typical curling of the foliage when mature. *N. triandrus* subsp. *capax* is a difficult bulb to find but it is well worth the effort.

This brings us to the end of the accepted wild forms of *N. triandrus,* but before we consider some of the very beautiful hybrids from *triandrus* 'blood,' I refer you once again to my earlier remarks about culture and the control of disease.

This group has been, for me at least, one of the most taxing and demanding to grow successfully. *The Daffodil Handbook* of the AHS notes as follows:

> *N. triandrus.* Distribution. Open grassy slopes and pine woods, on granite boulders and often on acid soil. Common on granitic hills.

This description suggests the need for exceptionally good drainage, which I believe to be essential. Yet those who have visited either Wisley or the Savill Gardens in England have seen colonies of these bulbs happily growing in a moist leafy soil under light woodland, and apparently doing very well indeed.

I have had trouble with every lot of bulbs I have purchased, especially when it was known to be collected material. Probably 15–20% die off from basal rot the first year no matter what is done and no matter how carefully they are grown. One clear exception has been the production of bulbs from my own seed, and in this case the bulbs appeared to be completely free of problems. With purchased stock I maintain what I loosely call kitchen cleanliness and the problems become less and less each year. However, so does the total number of bulbs! I have hopes that ultimately I may be able to select and establish selected, clean bulbs which will propagate by division, but in the meantime I sow seed each year.

The only wild form which so far has given me no trouble is *N. triandrus* subsp. *pallidulus* var. *aurantiacus* which originally came to me as cultivated bulbs from John Blanchard. However, he has since sent me others which I understand were collected and these too have grown without loss. But to be on the safe side when growing any kind of *N. triandrus* in pans, pay particular attention to additional drainage by adding more grit to the compost and surround the bulbs with pure grit as they are planted. Watch watering very carefully at all times, but especially after flowering when the bulbs have begun to die down.

Narcissus triandrus subsp. *triandrus* makes a delightful and decorative pan when well established.

Triandrus Hybrids

A substantial number of cultivars have been developed using *N. triandrus* as one of the parents, and almost without exception they are beautiful, well worth growing, but unfortunately many are not true miniatures. The principal form of *N. triandrus* used has been *N. triandrus* subsp. *capax.* This bulb is so clearly superior in every way that it has been the inevitable selection when making a *triandrus* cross.

'Agnes Harvey'. Katherine Spurrell. England. 1902. 5 W-W. 'Minnie Hume' × *N. triandrus* var. *albus* (now subsp. *triandrus*).

This is a very old cultivar which received an Award of Merit from the RHS in the year it was registered. It produces a clear white flower in late March under glass on a rather tall stem. Usually 9–12 in. (23–30 cm) tall it seems best suited to the miniature border in the garden where it grows very well. This is typical of the type of cultivar which, in my opinion, justifies the American Daffodil Society in establishing an Intermediate Class. Although the flower can be considered suitable for inclusion in the miniatures, the general habit of growth is closer to the standard than the miniature form.

'April Tears'. Alec Gray Camborne, England. 1939. 5 Y-Y. *N. jonquilla* × *N. triandrus* subsp. *concolor* (now *pallidulus*).

This is a first class bulb, and because it is so good, it has taken a rightful place as part of normal commercial bulb production. It is generally available each fall from

'April Tears'.
One of Alec Gray's
finest hybrids.

any good garden center. Flowers are produced as groups of 2–5 florets on 8–10 in. (20–25 cm) stems. A clump in the garden or in a pan is a splendid sight. However, although it can be grown with ease either inside or in the garden, the bulbs do not seem to thrive on continuous pan culture, so for best results a fresh pan of bulbs should be planted each autumn, the pan eventually being planted in the garden. This is really one of the best, all-purpose daffodils, quite up in the top of any list. No garden should be without it.

'Arctic Morn'. Alec Gray. Camborne, England. 1949. 5 W-W *N. triandrus* **subsp.** *loiseleuri* **(now subsp.** *capax***)** × **seedling 5 W-W**

When one reviews the list of miniature hybrids, Alec Gray's name is there from start to finish. 'Arctic Morn' is one of his many *triandrus* hybrids, using *N. triandrus* subsp. *capax* as one of the parents. The other parent is not known.

It is rather on the tall side—Gray says 6–8 in. (15–20 cm) but I have found it to grow somewhat taller, 8–10 in. (20–25 cm) in the greenhouse, and so I planted it outside. It produces 1–4 flowers per stem which are pure white, but which may have a hint of pink in the shallow cup. Grown outside this tint burns out quickly and may not be noticed.

'Arctic Morn'

'Cobweb'. Alec Gray. Camborne, England. 1938. 5 W-Y. *N. triandrus* **subsp.** *loiseleuri* **(now subsp.** *capax***)** × **seedling 5 W-W.**

I have not grown this but have reports that it is a poor grower and tends to fade away. Gray says that it is 10 in. (25 cm) tall, which suggests that it is only of value outdoors.

'Fairy Chimes'.
Close to April Tears,
but a very good bulb.

'Fairy Chimes'. Grant Mitch. Oregon. 1976. 5 Y-Y. *N. jonquilla* × *N. triandrus* var. *albus* **(now subsp.** *triandrus***).**

I have only recently obtained this bulb and flowered it for the first time. It is extremely close to 'April Tears' but with stems perhaps 10–12 in. (25–30 cm) i.e. about 2 in. (5 cm) taller. Although my bulbs have behaved normally so far, it is reputed to be a somewhat difficult bulb to grow. There seems little point in bothering with it if one already has 'April Tears' and 'Hawera,' both readily available.

'Frosty Morn'. Alec Gray. Camborne, England. 1941. 5 W-W. *N. triandrus* **subsp.** *loiseleuri* **(now subsp.** *capax***) cross.**

Gray described both this cultivar and 'Artic Morn' in his book in such a way as to suggest that he prefers 'Frosty Morn.' I certainly do for it is by far the better grower of the two for me. Gray's estimates of height are not always accurate for North America—he calls for 6 in. (15 cm) but mine have consistently been 8–10 in. (20–25 cm). It is pure white and has excellent substance, lasting in good condition for some time. It is best grown outside.

'Frosty Morn'. A better cultivar than 'Arctic Morn'.

'Hawera'. Dr. W. M. Thompson. New Zealand. 1938. 5 Y-Y. *N. jonquilla* × *N. triandrus* **var.** *albus* **(now subsp.** *triandrus***).**

There is confusion between this cultivar and 'April Tears' for they are very similar, and I regret to say, are often supplied one for the other by suppliers with poor ethical standards. To establish clearly the difference I made a collection from many sources, and sorted out the minor, but important, differences.

'Hawera' 5 Y-Y

This is by far the stronger grower of the two and usually comes into flower about two weeks ahead of 'April Tears.' The scapes (stems) are solid, round and from 12–14 in. (30–35 cm) tall when grown in pans in a cool greenhouse. The flowers on each stem are numerous, from 4–8, and slightly larger than 'April Tears.' The corona is distinctly larger although it tends to have a rather uneven edge. The color is lighter than 'April Tears.' On the RHS Color Chart it corresponds to CHINESE YELLOW HCC 606/2. The plant is more vigorous and might with reason be classed as an Intermediate. It is an excellent garden plant, growing and multiplying well.

'April Tears' 5 Y-Y

This cultivar comes into bloom at least ten days after 'Hawera.' It is similar in general appearance, but more delicate and less heavy. The flower stems are shorter, from 8–10 in. (20–25 cm). The truss is somewhat smaller, numbering from 2–4 flowers per scape. The color is distinctly different, being a darker yellow—BUTTERCUP YELLOW HCC 5/2. The cup is smaller with a less wavy edge—a smoother flower as Alec Gray describes it. The general effect is more that of a single tone color, while 'Hawera' makes one feel that it ought to be ramping away in the garden.

There is no question that these two bulbs are right at the top of the list of desirable miniatures, and as such are regularly grown by commercial growers and offered each fall. One cannot go wrong with either.

'Hawera'.
A similar cross to 'April Tears'.
This is the stronger grower.

'Icicle'. John Blanchard. Blandford, England. 1962. 5 W-W. *N. dubius* ×*N. triandrus* **var.** *loiseleuri* **(now subsp.** *capax*).

If someone were to say to me, "You must move, but you can take only one bulb with you," this is the one I would choose! Registered in 1962, only now is it becoming well-known and appreciated. As indeed it should be, for here is one that has everything. I have not yet attempted to grow it outside, but others tell me that it does as well in the miniature border. I have grown mine in pans and of the more than 300 pans that I have, this is tops, for it does well and has no problems with disease.

I received one bulb in 1981, and six more in 1982. I disposed of two leaving me with five. These have developed into sixteen good bulbs by 1985, which is really quite a good increase.

'Icicle' A single flower.

Planted late in August with the others, the bulb is rather slow in emerging. By the end of the year it can be seen, and by the end of January the foliage, which is glaucus, twisted and prostrate, is well over the pan. At the same time the first buds can just be seen, and although some color may be visible by mid-February, it really does not commence to flower in earnest until about March 1. By March 15, the pan is in full bloom and a sheer delight.

I usually rate my pans when in bloom on a scale of 1 to 4, 4 being the top of the scale. 'Icicle' is consistently marked as 5, i.e. outstanding. The flowers are pure white, produced in clusters of from 2–4 on each stem. Each flower is delicate, really crisp, crystalline white with a well-formed but modest cup. Flowering commences when the stems are only 2–3 in. (5–7.5 cm) high, but as the truss develops, the scape elongates to 5–7 in. (12.5–17.5 cm).

Unfortunately this cultivar is not yet widely available, and will be quite costly if it can be found. But if someone has a spare bulb, splurge and acquire it. No matter what one pays, one will be quite content.

'Little Lass'. Matthew Fowlds. U.S.A. 1969. 5 W-W. Small *cyclamineus* hybrid × *N. triandrus* var. *albus* (now subsp. *triandrus*).

This is a fine cultivar which is not yet listed as a miniature but which I think should be. This cross produced what is, in effect, a much larger and stronger form

'Little Lass'. A good cultivar which ought to be on the miniature list.

of *N. triandrus* var. *albus.* The scape is thick and eventually reaches 8–10 in. (20–25 cm) tall. Flowers are of a typical *triandrus* form, as large or even larger than *N. triandrus* subsp. *capax* and with quite large, strongly reflexed petals. It opens a pale cream and quickly fades to a pure white. It seems to be an excellent grower and does equally well indoors or out. I have had a bulb or two infected with stripe, so care must be taken to obtain bulbs which are clean.

'Raindrop'. Alec Gray. Camborn, England. 1942. 5 W-W. *N. triandrus* subsp. *capax* × *N. dubius.*

You will notice that this is the reciprocal cross which produced 'Icicle,' and the two are quite similar. Gray considered 'Raindrop' the finest miniature he produced, although I believe 'Tete-a-Tete' a more likely candidate.

Some years ago I received a small bulb of 'Raindrop' which produced only a single leaf for two years. On the third year three leaves came and eventually a small flower, which to my jaundiced eye did not appear to be outstanding. I could be wrong if and when the plant finally gets going, but so far, 'Icicle' seems to me to be infinitely better.

Gray describes it as a tiny polyanthus, 4–5 in. (10–12 cm) high with up to five snow-white flowers per stem. He writes of it but did not offer the bulb in his 1961 catalog. It seems that as desirable as this bulb might be, 'Icicle' is very similar and a much better grower.

'Sennocke'. Difficult to grow.

'Sennocke'. F. R. Waley. Sevenoakes, England. 1948. 5 Y-Y. Possibly *N. triandrus* **subsp.** *capax* × *N. minor.*

Mr. Waley is not certain as to the parentage of this cultivar, which apparently appeared spontaneously in his garden. It opens cream and fades to near white, and the flower is somewhat larger than most. In overall size and habit of growth it is similar to *N. minor* with stems 6–8 in. (15–20 cm) high. It does very well in pans, but when I planted out a group of apparently healthy bulbs they were all lost the first year to basal rot. I maintain one pan by careful culture indoors.

'Shrimp'. Alec Gray. Camborne, England. 1955. 5 Y-Y. *N. triandrus* **var.** *albus* **(now subsp.** *triandrus***)** × *N. requienii (juncifolius).*

This cultivar grows well but does not flower well. In six years my bulbs have flowered three times. When in bloom it is a pleasant miniature, with one, and sometimes two small, yellow flowers on 4 in. (10 cm) stems. It is interesting, but will never be among my top ten.

There are six more cultivars listed as miniature under Division 5 which I have not yet grown. They are:

'Cobweb'.Alec Gray, Camborne, England.1938.5 W-Y
'Doublebois'.Alec Gray, Camborne, England.1962.5 W-W
'Laura'.L. P. Detman, Australia.1979.5 W-W
'Lively Lady'.Alec Gray, Camborne, England.1969.5 W-W

'Mary Plumstead'.Alec Gray, Camborne, England.1966.5 Y-Y
'Poppet'.Alec Gray, Camborne, England.1958.5 W-W
Of these I have had reports of 'Mary Plumstead' as being a good bulb, very
similar in effect to 'April Tears.'

'Shrimp'. A delightful flower
but difficult to bring into bloom.

A new hybrid #82/47.
Narcissus triandrus subsp.
pallidulus × 'Pequineta'.

A new hybrid #82/49B. *Narcissus
triandrus* subsp. *triandrus* × *Narcissus
cantabricus* subsp. *petunioides*.

Narcissus cyclamineus. A superb species for pan culture.

CHAPTER NINE

Narcissus Cyclamineus

DIVISION 6

Narcissus cyclamineus

Although listed as a separate species in the Pseudonarcissus Section by Flora Europaea, it is so clearly different in every respect to others in the same Section that it has, by mutual consent, been treated on its own, and hybrids with a clear affinity with *N. cyclamineus* have been given a separate division, Division 6, in the classification of hybrids. This is the only species in the division, and is unique, well justifying the separate treatment accorded to it. Without doubt, it is one of the most attractive and valuable wild species, which fits most exactly and appropriately into the miniature daffodil world.

Moreover it has a most interesting and checkered history. It was clearly known and illustrated as far back as 1633, for an excellent line drawing of the complete flower and bulb appeared in the *Theatrum Florae* so clear and exact that there is no question as to its being authentic. Then somehow the bulb was lost and slowly over the next 200 years serious doubts arose as to its existence. In 1836, Dean Herbert presented a complete review of the AMARYLLIDACEAE in which he stated that *N. cyclamineus* was an "absurdity which will never be found to exist." Clearly the bulb was not in cultivation.

There the matter rested until 1885 when bulbs were again discovered near Oporto by Messrs. Tait and Schmitz. The Royal Horticultural Society in England awarded it a preliminary commendation in 1887 followed by a First Class Certificate later that year. From that time onwards *N. cyclamineus* has never looked back, providing the base for a valuable and interesting group of hybrids, many miniature and others of normal size, most being exceptionally fine and worthy of cultivation.

N. cyclamineus is unusual in that it is one of the very earliest of species in flower, generally at the same time as *N. asturiensis*. The leaves are quite distinct, being a bright fresh green completely lacking the glaucus tinge found on so many others. The stem is usually not more than 4–6 in. (10–15 cm) high and one flower only is produced per stem. The flower itself is quite unique. Always pendant, the corona is a long, narrow tube up to ¾ in. (20 mm) long, with petals about the same length strongly reflexed so that the line of the petals and corona are almost the same, i.e. reflexed 180°. The rim of the corona is usually slightly expanded and can be strongly serrated When grown in pans under glass the first flowers appear early in February, and the pan will be in full bloom by the third week. Flowers last a considerable time, some 3–4 weeks, a trait which *N. cyclamineus* has passed on to many of its progeny.

The bulbs prefer a rather moist soil with plenty of humus and do not take kindly to any degree of summer baking, which is essential for many other species. In fact the bulbs dislike being out of the ground for more than a few days, and thus the purchase of bulbs from any source presents a hazard. In recent years bulbs in the wild have been so heavily collected that it is now most difficult to find it growing naturally. Yet, up to the time of writing, most bulbs offered by European sources are collected material. This practice clearly cannot continue much longer, so they will either disappear from the market or some nurseryman will develop production from seed as a commercial enterprise. There is no reason why they should not be grown in this way, for if the flowers are self-pollinated, seed is usually set freely. The seed germinates without difficulty and in 3–4 years the plants grow to flowering size.

I had a modest amount of trouble with my original collected material due to basal rot, but it seems to be passing. Bulbs raised from seed have been clean and vigorous, and clearly this is the way to increase stocks, for division is at best, extremely slow.

Narcissus Cyclamineus Hybrids

The list of named hybrids now available in this division is somewhat larger than the one given by Gray, which clearly indicates the increased interest and activity in using *N. cyclamineus* for breeding during the past 30 years. I regret that in more than one instance I do not as yet have personal knowledge of some of these, but those that I do have are excellent, and one can thus presume, as I shall do, that most are well worth growing.

'Anticipation'. Alec Gray. Camborne, England. 1975. 6 Y-Y. *N. cyclamineus* × 'Tete-a-Tete'.

I have had this cultivar for two years and it has grown quite well. However, it is not on the Approved List of Miniatures and I can understand why. It produces a fairly substantial yellow flower of the typical *cyclamineus* form on stems from 10–12 in. (25–30 cm) high, and as such is just too large to be considered a true miniature. Planted outside it performs well, but I really cannot see any clear-cut improvement over many others. I consider it only average.

'Atom'. Grant E. Mitch. Oregon, U.S.A. 1975 6 Y-Y 'Wee Bee' × *N. cyclamineus*

In the three years I have had this bulb it has not flowered. Two years indoors and one outside still have not produced results. I said at the beginning that I thought most *cyclamineus* hybrids are worth growing, and then the first two mentioned do not seem to measure up. Certainly if 'Atom' does not begin to perform soon it will have to make way for something that does.

'Flute'. Alex Gray. Camborn, England. 1957. 6 Y-Y. 'Tanagra' × *N. cyclamineus*.

I have only just obtained this bulb and have not yet seen it bloom. Photographs indicate a slightly larger flower, typically cyclamineus.

'Flyaway'. Mrs. Geo. Watrous. Washington, D.C. U.S.A. 1964. 6 Y-Y. *N. Cyclamineus* × *N. jonquilla*.

Another cultivar I do not yet have. It is very well thought of by those who have it and in fact I have yet to hear of any bulb raised by Mrs. Watrous which is not worth growing.

'Humming Bird'

'Humming Bird'. Grant E. Mitch. Oregon, U.S.A. 1975. 6 Y-Y.

The parentage of this bulb is not clear. It appears to be an open pollinated seedling of *N. cyclamineus,* but with stems 6–8 in. (15–20 cm) tall. Whatever its parentage it is a very good bulb which I have now had for three years, growing without problems and flowering regularly. The flower is a rich deep yellow, very similar to *N. cyclamineus* but at least twice the size. In 1987 the first flowers opened on February 25 and were still in excellent condition on March 15. It is an excellent bulb.

'Jetage'. Alec Gray. Camborne, England. 1957. 6 Y-Y *N. cyclamineus* × **'Rockery White'.**

This is rather too tall for pan culture so it has been planted outside where it continues to flourish. Under normal conditions it comes into bloom towards the end of March and is another form closely resembling the original *N. cyclamineus* but larger in every way. The stems are at least 8–10 in. (20–25 cm) tall with the flower in proportion. It is very similar to 'Humming Bird' but the color is not quite so deep. It does very well.

'Jetfire'. Grant E. Mitch. Oregon, U.S.A. 1969. 6 Y-R. (('Market Merry' × 'Carbineer') ×
Armanda)) × *Cyclamineus*

I cannot pass this variety by, although it has no place in the miniature list because it is slightly too large. But what an excellent plant. I have a full pan in mid-February, with 9–12 in. (22.8 to 30 cm) stems upon which are fairly large flowers with the true *cyclamineus* appearance, reflexed petals and a rather long narrow

'Jetfire'. Although not a true miniature, this is a delight to grow in pans or garden.

corona. The petals are a clear yellow but the corona will be somewhat darker, even orange as it opens. As it matures it becomes deeper still until it has a rim of almost fiery red.

I grow it in pans, first because I like it and it performs well, and second I use it regularly to cross with other bulbs in the hope that somewhere in the future I will produce a true miniature with a clear red cup. Although 'Jetfire' cannot be classed as a miniature, I suggest you grow and enjoy it anyway.

'Jumblie'. Alec Gray. Camborne, England. 1952. 6 Y-O 'Cyclataz' selfed

This is a sibling of 'Quince' and 'Tete-a-Tete.' The account of how this group came about was recorded by Alec Gray in one of his last articles, published in the *RHS Daffodil Yearbook* of 1985-6. Gray notes that soon after the end of World War II, an unusual year occurred when seed was set on many bulbs which normally are completely sterile. He noticed that just one seed capsule had developed on a stem of 'Cyclataz' and when gathered, contained three seeds. These ultimately developed into three excellent bulbs, one of which he named 'Jumblie.'

'Jumblie' is very well named for the effect of the twin flowers can be a bit of a jumble. The stems are from 5–7 in. (12.5–17.5 cm) high on each of which may be produced one to three blooms. The color is a deep gold, with a strong hint of orange in the corona. The petals are reflexed after the form of *N. cyclamineus* but the corona is not so long. It can be grown with equal ease indoors or out, but as I also have 'Tete-a-Tete'indoors, I keep 'Jumblie' in the garden. It gives no trouble and is readily available at a reasonable price.

'Junior Miss'. Wm. G. Panill. Virginia, U.S.A. 1977. 6 W-Y. 'Jenny' × *N. jonquilla*.

White flowers in the *cyclamineus* Division are few and this plant is highly desirable. 'Jenny' being a *cyclamineus* hybrid has tranferred both the typical form and the white color. I do not yet have this, but hope to have it soon.

'Jumblie'. A good bulb for the garden.

'Kibitzer'. Mrs. Geo. Watrous. Washington D.C. U.S.A. 1968. 8 Y-Y. *N. minor* **var.** *conspicuus* × *N. cyclamineus.*

This is almost exactly the same cross as that recorded for 'Mini-cycla' which follows, and in fact when they are both in bloom it is hard to tell them apart, unless they are labelled. Both show buds early in February and by the third week of that month should be in full bloom. At maturity, 'Kibitzer' appears to develop the taller stem' up to 6 in. (15 cm) while 'Mini-cycla' matures at about 5 in. (12.5 cm). Both flowers are in effect a larger version of *N. cyclamineus* and of a deep rich yellow. I greatly enjoy them both.

'Kibitzer'. One of Mrs Watrous best. Fine in pans.

'Mini-cycla'. Not as hardy as Kibitzer.

'Mini-cycla'. F. Herbert Chapman. England. 1913. 6 Y-Y. *N. asturiensis* × *N. cyclamineus.*

It is good that these two cultivars come together in the list as I was tempted to lump them together. 'Mini-cycla' is still rather scarce although it was registered in 1913. There seems no obvious reason for this, excepting that perhaps it is not quite so hardy as some. As the leaves develop, a bud can be seen quite early in much the same manner as *N. asturiensis*, but the leaves are a bright fresh green after the manner of *N. cyclamineus*. Both this cultivar and 'Kibitzer' are ideal subjects for pan culture.

'Mite'. Sir J. A. R. Gore-Booth. England. 1965. 6 Y-Y. *N. pseudonarcissus* **subsp.** *obvallaris* × *N. cyclamineus.*

Yet another in the range of hybrids best described as a larger *cyclamineus*. With so many to choose from I have planted this one out in the garden, for with 7–8 in. (17.5–20 cm) stems it is slightly on the tall side for pan culture. It grows well in either place and is well worth having.

Although some of these bulbs may appear to be duplicates, there is a virtue in this, because not all bulbs perform well every year. One year 'Jetage' may do well, and on another 'Mite' is at its best. It pays to duplicate if one has the room.

'Mitzy'. Alec Gray. Camborne, England. 1955. 6 W-W. *N. cyclamineus* × **'Rockery White'.**

I like this cultivar because it is quite different from those already listed. Essen-

'Mite'. A bit tall for pans. Fine in the garden.

tially white, it does very well in pans and although slightly on the tall side, 6–8 in. (15–20 cm) I still grow it that way. The flowers produced in early February are about twice the size of *N. cyclamineus*. The long corona opens as a pale yellow and the petals, strongly reflexed, are quite white. As the flowers mature the color in the corona fades so the final effect is pure white. It really is a "dainty Miss" and one that is a pleasure to see. It has presented no disease problems, and increases by division steadily.

'Quince'. Alec Gray. Camborne, England. 1953. 6 Y-Y. Cyclataz selfed.
This is one of the three seedlings arising from that pod which appeared on 'Cyclataz.' Although interesting because of its history, I cannot see that it has any outstanding features. Gray says that it should be 4–6 in. (10–15 cm) but for me it has been consistently taller, close to 8 in.(20 cm). It usually produces more than one flower per stem, up to four which is an advantage. But the flowers seem somewhat muddled, not quite sure whether to be pure *N. cyclamineus* or 'Soleil d'Or.' It does appear to be reasonably hardy, more so than one might expect with *tazetta* blood in its makeup.

'Snipe'. A. M. Wilson. England. 1948. 6 W-W. 'W. P. Milner' × *N. cyclamineus.*
This is a beauty. Of typical *cyclamineus* form, but larger pure white flowers with the most dainty, reflexed petals. It is aptly named. Registered in 1948, I find it strange that it has not been more widely grown. Although not quite so small in stature as some of the others, growing perhaps 10 in. (25 cm) high in pans, it does not

'Mitzy'. Does well anywhere.

'Snipe'. Do not confuse with Jack Snipe. This is the one to grow.

seem to be out of place. At the end of February I always have a full 10 in. (25 cm) pan which may have at least 15 blooms delicately poised in a balanced and elegant manner.

The pan can with ease be placed in the center of a table for a formal dinner, where it is bound to be both a delight and a conversation piece. It grows outdoors with equal success. It is a quality cultivar which should be in every collection.

'Soltar' Alec Gray Camborne, England 1961 6 Y-Y

I list this cultivar to illustrate a point. It is described as a *N. cyclamineus* cross with yellow flowers. I ordered bulbs which when they bloomed were all white. What I received I do not know but clearly they were not 'Soltar.' I have yet to obtain this bulb, but disappointments and frustrations like this are common in miniature bulb growing. No one, but no one, seems to have genuinely true-to-name stock. Perhaps it is inherent in growing and handling these small bulbs. But be warned that if you start collecting you have to have tenacity beyond the norm to obtain what you want.

'Stella Turk'. A fine cultivar for pans. Lasts a long time in flower.

'Stella Turk'. Alec Gray. Camborne, England. 1958. 6 Y-Y. *N. calcicola* × *N. cyclamineus*.

Gray considered this a jonquilla type—Division 7—but it is listed in the Approved Miniature List as a Division 6. This is one of the best of the long list of Gray hybrids and one of the most successful cultivars I have grown.

Quite up to the level of 'Icicle,' it is a small, yellow trumpet with the corona shorter than most. The stems are short also, usually not more than 3–4 in. (7.5–10 cm) high. Bright green tufts of foliage are seen right after Christmas, and by the first of February buds can usually be seen in the center of each. By the beginning of March the first flowers open and the whole pan is in full bloom two weeks later. They remain fresh and unspoiled for weeks. Under the cool, temperate conditions of the greenhouse the first flowers last from three to four weeks, and with the natural spread of blooming, individual flowers can be found on the pan in good condition for up to six weeks. This seems to me to be an excellent value. The bulbs have given me no trouble at all. One bulb received in 1981 increased to 23 by 1985. It is first-class in every way and a true miniature for pan culture.

'Tete-a-Tete'.
Alec Gray's finest bulb.
Just an all round good cultivar.

'Tete-a-Tete'. Alec Gray. Camborne, England. 1949. 6 Y-O. N. 'Cyclataz' selfed.

There is no question that I am running out of adjectives! This, the third seed in the single pod of 'Cyclataz' produced a form which, without exaggeration has to head the list of all miniature bulbs in commercial production. Gray did not rate it too highly in the beginning, but the basic qualities of the bulb have brought it to the top, where I am sure it is certain to stay for many years. Why should this be? It is simply because the bulb is an excellent, all-round good grower, which can fit in almost anywhere and provide satisfactory results, whether it be forced for early flowers, grown cool in pots for mid-winter use, or planted in the garden with the rest. Wherever it is used, 'Tete-a-Tete' produces results.

It is a good, clear yellow with a stem length of from 6–8 in. (15–20 cm). The flowers may be produced singly, but are more frequently found in pairs, yet without the jumbled effect of 'Jumblie.' Because of its universal utility the bulb is now produced in the millions, and used and appreciated in countless ways, wherever daffodils are in demand. It is a first-class bulb, and readily available at a moderate cost.

This brings us to the end of the cyclamineus group. I am keenly conscious of a number of good bulbs which I have not listed because I have yet to grow them. These include:

'Flute'.Alec Gray.Camborne, England.1957.6 Y-Y
'Flyaway'.Mrs. Geo. Watrous.Washington D.C., U.S.A.1964.6 Y-Y
'Greenshank'.A. M. Wilson.England.1948.6 Y-Y
'Opening Bid'.Alec Gray.Camborne,England.1975.6 Y-Y
'Zip'.Grant E. Mitch.Oregon,U.S.A.1976.6 Y-Y

I have just received a bulb from New Zealand under the name 'Golden Snipe,' which I have yet to see in bloom. No parentage was given, but if it is a cultivar with the true 'Snipe' form, and a good yellow, it could be outstanding.

I have no doubt that when these cultivars become available most will be worth including in any collection, for, in the main, hybrids of *N. cyclamineus* seem destined to please.

CHAPTER TEN

The Jonquils

DIVISION 7

N. jonquilla is a plant that has been cultivated and appreciated for centuries. E. A. Bowles in his *Handbook of Narcissus* states that Clusius recorded and discussed a number of *jonquill* forms in his *Historia* published in 1601. Throughout the nearly 400 years since, jonquils have been described, appreciated, and above all treasured by emigrants who carried them to all parts of the world, and there cultivated them as a breath of home.

Unfortunately, despite this long history, no one is completely satisfied as to what is what. Thirty years ago Gray opened his discussion of the jonquils with the following:

The various species are not always easy to distinguish, and

there is some confusion amongst writers on the subject.

Recently, John Blanchard, writing in the 1981–2 *Daffodil Yearbook* of the RHS commences the *Section Jonquillae* as follows:

The jonquils can be difficult to identify as the species tend to

merge into one another.

I have decided that I will not add to the confusion, and, without botanical argument, simply divide the species into four groups, following Grays lead as follows:

Group 1 Plants medium in height, 6–10 in. (20–25 cm).
Multiple flowers per stem.

N. jonquilla	yellow
N. jonquilla 'Flora pleno'	double yellow
N. fernandesii	yellow
N. willkommii	yellow

Group 2 Plants tall 9–12 in. (22.8–30 cm).
Multiple flowers per stem.

N. henriquesii	yellow
N. requienii	yellow

Group 3 Plants small. 4–6 in. (10–15 cm).
Several flowers per stem.

N. calcicola	yellow
N. scaberulus	yellow

Group 4 Plants small. 4–6 in. (10–15 cm).
Single flowers per stem.

N. atlanticus	creamy white

N. cuatrecasasii	yellow
N. gaditanus	yellow
N. marvieri	yellow
N. rupicola	yellow
N. watieri	white

Group 1

Plants medium in height 6–10 in. (20–25 cm). Multiple flowers per stem. I have chosen this as Group 1 because it contains the bulb from which the division gets its name.

N. jonquilla

As might be expected there are numerous variations on the type, some smaller, some larger, and some previously considered as individuals, but now submerged under this heading. The typical plant produces a tuft of deep green leaves, almost cylindrical in form, and ultimately a flower scape 9–12 in. (22.5–30 cm) tall. The bright, deep yellow flowers are produced in groups of 2–5 per stem and are strongly fragrant.

I have received from different sources bulbs named Arkansas Jonquil and Louisiana Jonquil, which when they flower seem identical to the basic type. These bulbs with localized names are, I presume, bulbs brought originally from Europe and now quite often naturalized. Southern forms do seem to be slightly more precocious in commencing growth in the fall, but apart from this the final result is the same. All jonquils are easy to grow and do best in light, well-drained soil and plenty of sun. The bulbs are dark brown, sometimes almost black and do not appear to be unduly subject to the basal rot diseases.

N. jonquilla var *minor* see *N. willkommii*

N. jonquilliodes see *N. willkommii*

N. jonquilla. 'Flora Pleno'.

Colloquially known as 'Queen Ann's Jonquil' this also is an extremely old cultivar, retained here and there in private gardens but never becoming really popular. Alec Gray found some growing in a Cornish garden called Pencrebar and reintroduced the bulb under that name in 1929. The flowers open a small, golden ball of multiple petals, but it just will not flower in pans and does so occasionally in the garden. It is interesting only as a historical oddity.

N. juncifolius see *N. requienii*

N. fernandesii. 10 Y-Y.

Introduced as recently as 1948, this species is an excellent form of jonquil, medium in height, 6–8 in. (15–20 cm), with semi prostrate foliage. Bright yellow, multiple flowers are produced on cylindrical stems about 6 in. (15 cm) high. It does very well in pans coming into bloom towards the end of February. It gives little or no trouble with disease. It is a good bulb.

N. willkommii. 10 Y-Y.

This is the last in Group 1 and a most delightful species it is. Rather smaller than the other two, it is slight in form and daintier. Two or three flowers are usually

Narcissus jonquilla. **Photographed in the wild.**

produced on a thin stem perhaps 6 in. (15 cm) tall and it does as well for me in pans or outside. Reputed to be difficult to bloom, I have not found it so. I suspect that what it needs is slightly better growing conditions if it is to flower well. One of the latest to bloom, the pan is in full bloom by mid-March, and similarly outside about a month later.

Group 2

> Plants tall 9–12 in. (22.8–30 cm)
> Multiple flowers per stem.

N. henriquesii 10 Y-Y

For some reason this species is not recorded in *Flora Europaea,* yet in my opinion it is one of the best in the entire group. It is the form preferred by most hybridizers when a good jonquil form is needed. The plant is taller than all the others, and is questionably a true miniature. The foliage tends to be round and rush-like as do many others, and reaches a height of 12–14 in. (30–40 cm). The leaves remain more or less upright as contrasted to *N. fernandesii* in which the foliage is shorter and semi prostrate. The smooth, tubular flower stems are 10–12 in. (25–30 cm) high and the flowers are usually borne in multiples of 3–5. The color is a fine, clear yellow and as with most jonquils, there is a strong fragrance. Stocks as received contained some basal rot, but this is cleared up by careful attention after which the bulbs seem to be without problems. I have used it as a parent but so far without success. When fertilized with another form, seed is set; but the seedlings prove to be straight *henriquesii* when they flower so must be presumed to be parthenocarpic. But it has been used successfully by others as a parent to good effect. I have not yet grown bulbs outside, but I feel sure that they would succeed without difficulty.

Narcissus henriquesii.
A first class jonquil species.

Plate 5. 1, *Narcissus rupicola*; **2**, *N. watieri*; **3**, *N. calcicola*; **4**, *N. scaberulus*; **5**, *N. marvieri*: **6**. *N. atlanticus*; **7**, *N. reauienii*.

Narcissus requienii (juncifolius).

N. requienii. **10 Y-Y.**

For years this bulb has been grown under the name *N. juncifolius* but *Flora Europaea* states that it should now be known as *N. requienii.* Having accepted this change with some reluctance, now comes word that the name should be changed again! This latest suggestion, which to my simple mind seems quite unnecessary, even ludicrous, I shall resist.

Although it has been known and grown for a very long time, I am not absolutely certain that the bulb I am growing is true to name. This stock came from the RHS in England, and I shall consider it true until I am shown clearly that it is not. Unfortunately, I have four other bulbs from other sources, all slightly different, all reputed to be *N. requienii* and none of them exactly the same as those obtained from the RHS.

This last is, however, an excellent bulb, somewhat similar to *N. henriquesii* in size and form with stems from 10–12 in. (25–30 cm) high. It is the first of the jonquils to flower in the greenhouse. Buds can usually be seen in late November and soon after the first of the year it is in full bloom. Stems have two flowers on each, bright yellow, with a deeper yellow cup. It is strongly fragrant. A month later, in early February, most of the flowers will still be in good condition, after which the pan slowly declines until flowering is finished in late February. The foliage is stiff, upright, and typically jonquil in form.

I have had no problems with disease and the bulbs multiply readily. Although I have not tried it outdoors, I am sure that it will be excellent. This seems to be the best form of *N. requienii.* The others may well be collections made from different areas. If so, none have, as yet, proved superior to the RHS form.

Narcissus calcicola

Group 3

Plants small 4–6 in. (10–15 cm)
Several flowers per stem.

N. calcicola

Another species for which I have multiple specimens, all somewhat similar and all slightly different. One of the best is a bulb which is smaller than any so far mentioned. It commences to bud in mid-January and is usually in flower by the end of February. Two or more flowers are produced on 6–7 in. (15–18 cm) stems. The flowers are bright yellow, and have a small, round, well-formed cup. When I have grown enough to fill a pan, the result will be one of those ideal bulbs which fall naturally into the miniature category. There have been no cultural problems to date.

N. scaberulus. 10 Y-Y.

Once considered a rarity, this is now more generally available. It is a delightful bulb, but like all the others, extremely variable. The foliage is glaucus, usually erect and from 6–7 in. (15–18 cm) tall. In most batches of collected bulbs, many grow with almost completely prostrate foliage, similar to some forms of *N. triandrus*. I have separated these but there seems no difference in the flowers. The stems are usually from 4–6 in. (10–15 cm) tall, and there can be 2–4 flowers on each stem. Individual flowers are quite small, not more than ½ in. (12 mm) wide, bright yellow with a deeper orange cup. It is a charming little bulb, flowering in late February indoors.

I did have cultural problems with this species when first received. Losses from basal rot were high, but the problem was corrected by growing the bulbs in a pocket of sand—see details under *N. triandrus*. This cleared things up and now I have no trouble. The special planting method is, however, continued. It seeds readily and bulbs grown from seed develop quickly and without trouble. I have found this to be true for many of the species. Purchased bulbs, usually collected, may suffer heavy losses in the beginning, but if seed can be set and grown to maturity under clean conditions, these bulbs grow without trouble or loss.

N. scaberulus Grazalema form. see N. cuatrecasasii.

Narcissus scaberulus

Group 4

Plants small 4–6 in. (10–15 cm)
Single flowers per stem.

N. atlanticus

This fairly recent introduction comes from the Atlas Mountains in Morocco and is one of the two jonquil species which is white. The bulbs are larger than some, and the foliage broader, eventually reaching a length of 8–10 in. (20–55 cm). The stem is slightly shorter usually 6–7 in. (15–18 cm), and the flowers are 1 in. (2.5 cm) across. The color is a creamy white. The general effect is not quite so attractive as the other white jonquil species, *N. watieri.*

The introduction to cultivation of this species has quite an interesting history. Seed was gathered by E. K. Balls, a well known plant collector, in 1936, and grown to maturity by Col. F. C. Stern, who exhibited it and published a description in 1950. Since that time many people have tried to find the original site in the Amiziz area of Morocco but without success. All the bulbs which are now being grown have originated from that initial seed collection. I grow it because white forms are rare and it is useful for hybridizing. However, *N. watieri* is clearly more desirable.

Narcissus atlanticus

N. cuatrecasasii 10 Y-Y.

Yet one more species with a checkered career. Originally collected near Grazalema in Spain by Commander Stocken, it was introduced as *N. scaberulus* Grazalema form. Eventually the botanists felt that it ought to be listed as *N. rupicola* subsp. *pedunculatus* but now *Flora Europaea* says that it should be given specific status as N. cuatrecasasii. So, is the bulb worth all this trouble? I think not. In effect it is very similar to *N. rupicola.* q.v. but does not grow at all easily or flower well. I have had bulbs for six years which have only flowered twice. Seven bulbs planted last year did not flower at all. When it does flower the blooms are produced in early

Narcissus cuatrecasasii

March on 4–5 in. (10–12.5 cm) stems. The flowers are yellow and closely resemble N. rupicola.

Since writing the above I have received two further collections from the wild which do not look the same. One is distinctly more robust, appears to grow without difficulty, and is budding well in late February. Final judgment must wait upon the performance of this bulb, but the original form is not a bulb I would strive to obtain. The second I have just received from Michael Salmon under the name *N. cuatrecasasii* var. *segimonensis*, collected recently at Cabra in Spain. It will be interesting to see how this collection differs from those already on hand.

Narcissus gaditanus

N. gaditanus. 10 Y-Y.

I would assume that this has to be the absolute smallest daffodil species, for it is delicate and minute in every detail. Quite easy to grow, the bulbs flourish and split to such a marked degree that to find a bulb as large as a peanut is exceptional. Many are no larger than a good-sized grain of rice. The foliage is extremely thin—filiform—and lies flat on top of the pan. Year after year that is all it does—produce a mat of thin, fine foliage.

John Blanchard gave me my original stock, reporting that he had grown it for 10 years before he obtained a flower. It was no doubt beginner's luck, but the second year my pan produced 15 flowers, since then, none. The flower is very small, not more than ⅜ in. (10 mm) in diameter and is interesting only as an oddity. On the one occasion when the bulbs flowered for John Blanchard, he made a number of crosses, some of which I have. To date all these seem to have retained most of the poor qualities of *N. gaditanus*, including heavy splitting, and a tendency not to flower or to do so sparsely. Apart from being a challenge to bring into flower, it appears to be of little value.

N. minutiflorus see N. gaditanus

N. rupicola. **10 Y-Y.**

Here is a species I like very much indeed. Coming from Spain many different forms have been collected. I have three at present, labelled small, medium and large. The principal differences are the height of the stem and the width of flower. For some years now, bulbs obtained from Europe as collected material under the name *N. juncifolius* have, without exception, been *N. rupicola,* so a number of growers have this bulb, but under the wrong name. *N. rupicola* has a bulb which when well grown, is slightly larger than many, and with a rather pale skin. It is late in commencing growth, so leaves may not appear till late in November. The stiff, upright foliage is usually 5–7 in. (12–17 cm) high and glaucus. Buds do not appear till February and the pan is usually in full bloom in mid-March. This makes it just about the last of the true miniature species to come into bloom. The solitary flowers are flat and 1 in. (2.5 cm) or more in width. Well-established bulbs, growing well, may have flowers 1½ in. (3.7 cm) or more in width, while the so-called large form has flowers nearly twice this size, and with a well defined cup. Flower stems range from 4 in. (10 cm) to 8 or 9 in. (20–22.8 cm) on the largest forms. The color on all of these is a clear bright yellow. Seed is set regularly and with ease, and bulbs raised from self-pollinated seed do very well indeed.

The only problem I have had is in the first two or three years when cleaning up collected material. On a number of occasions I have lost up to 40% the first year, but, as with most bulbs, the losses dwindle, until I finally have a residue of strong, healthy bulbs. Clearly the best way to increase stock is by seed.

Narcissus rupicola

Plate 6. 1, *Narcissus fernandesii*; 2, *N. cordobensis*; 3, *N. jonquilla*; 4, *N. willkommii*; 5, *N. henriquesii*; 6, *N. baeticus*; 7, *N. gaditanus*; 8, *N. viridiflorus*.

Comparison. Left, *Narcissus rupicola* subsp. *marvieri*; right, *Narcissus rupicola*.

N. rupicola subsp. marvieri. 10 Y-Y.

Although this is considered as a form of *N. rupicola*, it is often listed simply under the name *N. marvieri*. It is a larger flowered, and presumably a superior form of *N. rupicola* which originates in North Africa. Growing in much the same manner as *N. rupicola*, the foliage is not glaucus, and the final result is a plant somewhat larger than *N. rupicola* in all its parts. Foliage will usually reach 8 in. (20 cm) and the flower stems will be as tall. The flower, clearly larger than the general run of *N. rupicola*, is generally more robust.

I have had both good and bad stocks of this bulb. The first lot proved to be a complete disaster in which most of the bulbs rotted. I threw the few remaining away. A second batch from another source proved quite the opposite, and although I lost two bulbs of 14 planted this still seemed quite good. Now only an occasional bulb is lost, and that usually due to careless watering after flowering is completed. This species does require the special planting treatment—see *N. triandrus*—the bulbs being placed in a layer of sand. Last year I planted 28, some very small, and harvested 33 good sound bulbs.

N. rupicola subsp pedunculatus see N. cuatrecasasii

N. watieri. 10 W-W.

This, the last of the species, should in fact be first, for it is in every way a delightful plant. Very similar to *N. rupicola* in size and form, the flowers are of the purest crispest white imaginable. Alec Gray puts it this way:

The flowers are of the purest frosty white, so white indeed
that they make every other narcissus look 'off white' or cream.

Quite dwarf, the foliage is stiffly upright with a glaucus tinge and reaches perhaps 6 in. (15 cm) in height. The flower stems are slightly shorter and upon each is a single flower, measuring 1½–1¾ in. (3.5–4 cm) in width. A pan in full bloom is as good as a pan of *N. petunioides* or 'Icicle.' However, there has to be some snag—the bulb is quite susceptible to basal rot if not treated with care. Strangely, I have not found it necessary to plant the bulbs in sand as with many others. A normal com-

Narcissus watieri   *Narcissus cordobensis*

post and the generous use of the mixed fungicide powder (see Chapter 5) seems to do the trick. Although the compost must be well-drained. I have better results from a compost on the rich side, relying upon the heavy dressing of fungicide powder for protection. As might be imagined, *N. watieri* has been widely used for hybridizing as we shall see when we consider hybrids.

Last year I received bulbs from Michael Salmon of two forms of *N. jonquilla.* The first was *N. baeticus,* which did not flower. Salmon records it as a new species of medium size, all yellow, and with a wide and shallow cup. The second, now named *N. cordobensis,* had previously been distributed as a form of jonquilla from Antiquerra and Grazalema in Spain. This did flower and it looks most interesting. Buds were seen in late December and opened early in January. At the end of that month I recorded that it was still in bloom and in good condition. The stems are rather tall, 12–15 in. (30–38 cm) and the flowers, bright yellow and fragrant, were unusual in that the six petals were distinctly separate giving it the effect of a small windmill. Two to four flowers appeared on each stem. I noted at the time, "This is a very nice flower." It should be tried outside, for it is too tall for pan culture.

Narcissus Jonquil Hybrids

Hybridizing of the miniature Jonquils has been quite active and the current A.D.S. Approved List of Miniatures lists 28 cultivars. They are immensely popular and many enthusiasts appear to prefer any form of jonquil to almost all other species. They do have certain clear advantages, including delicate form, ease of indoor culture, and sometimes intense fragrance. As a group they tend to bloom later than many which prolongs the season. These qualities have clearly been appealing to past generations, for the generic name jonquil has been applied, and is still applied by some, to all narcissus.

The culture of narcissus is an extremely ancient activity. E. A. Bowles in *Handbook of Narcissus* notes that the earliest reference to any form of narcissus appears to be that of Theophrastus who wrote his *Enquiry into Plants* about the year 300 B.C. Theophrastus mentions three forms, one of which is almost certainly *N. tazetta.*

1900 years later in 1629, John Parkinson in his *Paradisus* discussed a number of forms of jonquil, so it seems clear that this section of the genus *Narcissus* has held a prominent position for well over 2000 years. Reviewing the list of cultivars, I feel that some selection is needed, for many are very similar to each other, with only minor differences of little importance. All will be listed, but I write in detail only about those really worth having.

'Baby Moon'. J. Gerritsen & Son. Holland, 1958. 7 Y-Y. *N. jonquilla* **var.** *minor* × *N. jonquilla.*

This cultivar and 'Baby Star' both come from Gerritsen and I wonder why both were selected. One would be sufficient. Both are small forms of the typical jonquil, and appear very similar to *N. willkommii*. They both do better in the garden than in pans and are one of the latest cultivars to bloom. Small, bright yellow, jonquil-type flowers are produced on 5–6 in. (12–15 cm) stems in late April. They are good for the miniature border or the rock garden.

'Baby Star'. J. Gerritsen. Holland. 1959. 7 Y-Y. *N. jonquilla* **var.** *minor* × *N. jonquilla.*
See the comments for 'Baby Moon'

'Bebop'. Alec Gray. Camborne, England. 1949. 7 W-Y. *N. rupicola* × *N. poeticus.*

This is the first, alphabetically, of a group of hybrids originated by Alec Gray which are all first-class bulbs, and highly desirable for the miniature border. They are just a few inches too tall for good pan culture but are ideal for the garden. We will consider this one in more detail and refer the others back to this description.

Individual bulbs are somewhat larger than most miniatures. They are slow to

'Bebop'. See also 'Sundial' on page 27.

commence growth, not appearing above ground in pans until the end of January. They are similarly late outside. Foliage is quite heavy, and of the traditional narcissus-form, eventually reaching a height of 8–10 in. (20–25 cm). Individual flowers are freely produced on 6–8 in. (15–20 cm) stems. The flowers are flat, usually slightly more than 1 in. (2.5 cm) across with pale cream petals and a small yellow cup. It settles down well in the garden, eventually forming a dense clump, from which many flowers are produced. Occasional lifting and replanting may be required, but I have had a fine clump in place for five years and it is still blooming well. There have been no problems with disease.

This cultivar, typical of the group, is an excellent bulb, and because it grows well is usually available each year form Dutch suppliers. One or more of this group can usually be found on the shelves of any good garden center.

'Bobbysoxer'. Alec Gray. Camborne, England. 1949. 7 YYO. *N. rupicola* × *N. poeticus*.
From the same cross as 'Bebop'. Slightly taller with flower stems 8–10 in. (20–25 cm). The petals are a butter-yellow but the cup is a bright orange. It flowers somewhat later than 'Bebop,' but is just as good in every way.

'Chit Chat'. Matthew Fowlds. U.S.A. 1975. 7 Y-Y. *N. requienii* × *N. jonquilla*.
One of a number of similar cultivars, usually from the same cross. It is a small, bright yellow jonquil, which flowers profusely once it has settled down. Although it will grow fairly well in pans, it seems best in the garden. No problems with disease. Slightly taller, 7–8 in. (17.5–20 cm), than 'Baby Moon' or 'Baby Star,' the flowers are somewhat similar.

'Clare'. Alec Gray. Camborne, England. 1968. 7 Y-Y. *N. rupicola* × *N. poeticus*.
Although registered later than the others this must have come from the same cross as 'Bebop.' It is an excellent cultivar and flowers at about the same time as the

'Clare'

group. Slightly taller—perhaps up to 8–10 in. (20–25 cm)—it grows exceptionally well in the garden, forming a solid clump which produces flowers profusely year after year. The color is a uniform lemon-yellow, and each flower is at least 1 in. (2.5 cm) across.

'Curleylocks'. Mrs. G. Watrous. Washington, D.C. U.S.A. 1964. 7 Y-Y. 'Seville' × *N. requienii*

I have not grown this bulb but anything that Mrs. Watrous releases is likely to be good. I am on the lookout for a bulb.

'Demure'. Alec Gray. Camborne, England. 1953. 7 W-Y. *N. watieri* × ?

Gray does not give the second parent but describes it as "A very refined, little flower," which it most certainly is. I began growing this cultivar, as I do with every bulb, in a pan, but after one year decided that it should go outside. There it has continued to prosper, but grows and divides more slowly than other Gray hybrids, such as 'Bebop.' 6–8 in. (16–20 cm) high, the petals are milk-white, with a small pale yellow cup in the center. It is in every way refined, but for a "riot of color" this is not the bulb. It will always remain a quiet delight.

'Flomay'. Alec Gray. Camborne, England. 1946. 7 W-WPP. *N. watieri* × ?

Named for Mrs. Gray, this is one of the very few white cultivars in this section. The stems are not usually more than 4–6 in. (10–15 cm) tall and the solitary flowers are about ¾ in. (2 cm) across. Gray says that the edge of the cup is faintly edged with a pinkish buff color, but this is hard to see. Nevertheless, it is a nice cultivar and worth cultivation, due to its unusual color. I have not found it too easy, and have lost some bulbs to basal rot. However, this could have been due to the fact that the bulbs came to me diseased, because, now that I have had some bulbs for three years, the trouble seems to have abated.

'Heide'. Matthew Fowlds. USA. 1975. 7 Y-Y. *N. requienii (juncifolius)* × *N. jonquilla*.

Although this cultivar was introduced in 1975 it seems to have dropped out of sight. I do not have it so cannot make any comments.

'Hifi'. Alec Gray. Camborne, England. 1959. 7 Y-Y. *N. calcicola* × yellow trumpet.

This sounds an unusual cross. Again, I regret I do not have this bulb, but I've heard good reports from other growers.

'Kidling'. Alec Gray. Camborne, England. 1951. 7 Y-Y. *N. jonquilla* × *N. requienii (Juncifolius)*.

In 1962 I obtained a number of bulbs for the first time and among them was this cultivar. I liked it immediately and have grown and enjoyed it ever since. Similar to 'Baby Moon' and 'Chit 'Chat,' 'Kidling' seems to have an additional air of quality lacking in many. It does very well in pans, and in the garden, producing abundant flowers on 6 in. (15 cm) stems. It does tend to split rather too much, but slightly deeper planting helps. All are late blooming, with bright yellow flowers and a strong fragrance.

'Little Prince'. Barr and Sons. England. 1937. 7 Y-O. *N. requienii (juncifolius* × *N. poeticus).*

I do not have this bulb and have heard no comments about it although it is on the current miniature list.

'Kidling'. One of the best in Alec Gray's long list of jonquil hybrids.

'Pencrebar'

'Pease-blossom' **Alec Gray. Camborne, England. 1961. 7 Y-Y.** *N. juncifolius* **(now**
requienii) × *N. triandrus albus* **(now** *N. triandrus* **subsp.** *triandrus*)**.**

I thought I had this cultivar and have been carefully nurturing a pan for the
past four years. This year, finally, I had a single flower of poor form and a dirty
white. Clearly this is not 'Peaseblossom,' for Gray describes it as 4 in. (10 cm) high
with 1–3 dainty little flowers on each stem. It sounds exciting and I want it, for the
cross sounds unusual.

'Pencrebar.' **Alec Gray. Camborne, England. 1929. 4 Y-Y.**

Being a double-flower this cultivar is placed in Division 4, but I have included
it here because it is a jonquil. It is one of the few double-flowers which do reasonably well. Even so, not in pans but in the garden only. Gray registered this form in
1929, noting that it was found by H. G. Hawker in an old Cornish garden. The
flowers are truly double, produced quite late in the season on 6–8 in. (15–20 cm)
stems. The old name for this bulb is Queen Anne's Double Jonquil, referring in this
instance to Queen Anne of England. Queen Anne's Double Daffodil is 'N.
eystettensis' and in this instance the name refers to Queen Anne of Austria. Bulbs
of 'Pencrebar' can occasionally revert from double to single flowers in the garden.

'Pequineta'. John Blanchard. Blandford, England. 1984. 7 Y-Y. *N. atlanticus* × *N.*
cuatrecasasii **(56–7c).**

One of the latest, and one of the very best of the Division 7 miniatures. First
selected by John Blanchard in 1956, two years ago he decided that this plant
deserved to be registered and named.

It is a first-class bulb, easy to grow, flowering regularly and profusely. In pans
it is slow to start, usually not being seen above ground before the new year. By the
end of February it should be budding, and in full bloom by the middle of March.
The stems are on the tall side, i.e. 7–8 in. (17–20 cm), and the flowers are born

'Pequineta'. The first, and one of the best new jonquil hybrids from John Blanchard.

singly. Each is a very well-formed flower, perhaps 1–1½ in. (2.5–4 cm) across, deep yellow with a small cup. The petals are somewhat overlapped which gives the flower a very smooth character. It is delightfully fragrant.

I have had this bulb for six years now, and it clearly is one of the best of the new hybrids. It does not appear to be subject to disease in any unusual way. The bulbs grow and multiply in a most satisfactory manner and should be available from good specialist suppliers. Still rather expensive, it is well worth the money. I have not yet tried the bulb outside but believe that it should be excellent there also.

'Pixie'. Matthew Fowlds. U.S.A. 1959. 7 Y-Y. *N. requienii (juncifolius)* × *N. jonquilla.*
I have not grown this cultivar. It appears to be one of the many, quite similar to each other, of which 'Chit Chat' and 'Kidling' are typical. One hardly needs them all.

'Pixie's Sister'. Grant Mitch. Oregon, U.S.A. 1966. 7 Y-Y. *N. requienii (juncifolius)* × *N. jonquilla*
This cultivar performs quite well in both pan and border. The small flowers are produced on 5–6 in. (12.5–15 cm) stems in twos and threes. Mitch says this is quite close to 'Chit Chat' and he is right. The only reason for growing some of these duplications is the chance that one cultivar may prove to be a better grower than the others. In this respect 'Pixies Sister' is only average.

'Rikki'. Alec Gray. Camborne, England. 1962. 7 W-Y. *N. watieri* × *N. poeticus.*
One or two growers who list this cultivar call for it to be 6 in. (15 cm) but for me it has consistently grown 8–10 in. (20–25 cm) and at this height quickly found it place in the garden. But there it is fine and grows well. The flower is larger than many, 1½ in (2.5–4 cm) across. The petals are almost white, and the small cup a clear yellow. It is a good bulb for the miniature border.

'Sea Gift'. Alec Gray. Camborne, England. 1935. 7 Y-Y.
This is a true, natural miniature jonquil, with flowers of the typical jonquil color, slightly smaller than the standard type, produced on 6–7 in. (15–17.5 cm) stems. Gray says that he found it growing in a Cornish garden and believes it to be of Spanish origin.

There is a folk-tale which supports this idea. It seems that a Spanish ship ran aground on the Cornish coast. One of the sailors was rescued and ultimately nursed back to health by a Cornish fisherman and his wife. When leaving for home he promised to send a gift to the lady of the house, and in due time a parcel of bulbs arrived. This tale suggested the name which Gray gave to it. The plant is a pleasant one, grows well, but is not outstanding in any way. Simply a nice bulb to have, with a little extra "history" attached.

'Skiffle'. Alec Gray. Camborne, England. 1957. 7 Y-Y. *N. asturiensis* × *N. calcicola.*
I received bulbs supposed to be 'Skiffle' but they were not true, so I do not yet have it. Gray says that it is a bright little jonquil with one or two flowers on each stem and that it flowers early. It sounds nice, for he says that it is only 3 in. (7.6 cm) tall.

'Stafford'. Alec Gray. Camborne, England. 1956. 7 Y-O. *N. rupicola* × *N. poeticus.*
One of the 'Bebop' group, and very similar in many respects. Flower stems are usually 7–8 in. (17.5 cm) tall and the flowers are fairly large and quite flat. The

petals are a light yellow, and the cup a bright orange. After a year in pans where it was clearly too tall, I planted it outdoors and it has grown very well. The foliage tends to be prostrate and although it is supposed to be early-flowering, mine came in with all the rest in the middle of March.

'Sundial'. Alec Gray. Camborne, England. 1955. 7 Y-Y. *N. rupicola* × *N. poeticus.*

Somewhat similar to 'Bobbysoxer' but much earlier flowering. Gray notes that this is more dwarf than others in the 'Bebop' group but this is not obvious here in my garden. Its early flowering habit is of value for it avoids duplication. The flower is a flat and uniform yellow, including the cup. The entire flower is like a yellow dial; hence the name. Flowers are usually produced two to a stem, as opposed to single flowers on most of the others in the group.

'Sun Disc'. Alec Gray. Camborne, England. 1946. 7 Y-Y. *N. rupicola* × *N. poeticus.*

It should be noted that this comes from the same cross as 'Sundial,' and the two cultivars are quite similar in a number of ways. Flowering a little later, the flowers are produced singly. The petals are a light yellow and the cup a deep, clear yellow so that it stands out as a deep-colored disc in the center of the flower. Because both this bulb and 'Sundial' have proven to be such good growers, they have become standard commercial cultivars, produced in quantity by the Dutch growers. Both are usually easily available from most good garden centers at a moderate cost.

'Wideawake'. Mrs. Geo. Watrous. Washington DC, U.S.A. 1964. 7 Y-Y. 'Seville' × *N. requienii (juncifolius).*

A second selection by Mrs. Watrous from the same cross as 'Curleylocks,' and another that I do not have. In some ways it seems easier to obtain bulbs from the other side of the world than right next door. Or is it that the grass in the distance appears greener? But I will have it soon I hope, for it sounds an interesting cross.

This brings us to the end of the list of more or less readily available jonquil

'Moncorvo'. The second new hybrid in this range from John Blanchard.

'Sabrosa'. Third in line. All are excellent bulbs.

hybrids. Just recently, two new cultivars have been registered by John Blanchard and should be mentioned as bulbs which we hope will soon be available. They are:

'Moncorvo'. John Blanchard. Blandford, England. 1986. 7 Y-Y.

N. henriquesii × *N. watieri* (71-3B).

'Sabrosa'. John Blanchard. Blandford, England. 1986. 7 Y-Y.

N. henriquesii × *N. watieri* (71-3D).

I have both of these but it is too soon to tell just how good they may be. However, first impressions are that they will be excellent for they grow well, without difficulty and flower regularly. I have in the past stressed the value which I place on what I call a "good doer." This quality is particularly noticeable in all of the newer Blanchard hybrids, such as the two above and 'Pequinita'. It is also an important characteristic of most of the truly popular and well known miniatures, such as 'Tete-a-Tete' and 'Hawera.' For this reason, I feel that a bright future lies ahead for these new Blanchard hybrids. 'Lintie,' which is an old cultivar registered in 1937, has recently been removed form the Approved List of Miniatures, as indeed it should be for it is just too tall. 'Pipers Barn,' another Gray hybrid, is still being grown in England but is not on the approved list.

CHAPTER ELEVEN

Narcissus Tazetta and Narcissus Poeticus

DIVISIONS 8 AND 9

N. tazetta

Division 8 has few species which fall into the miniature category, and the selection of hybrids is equally reduced. *N. tazetta* is the basic form, found generally around the perimeter of the Mediterranean, and from which have come many selected cultivars grown mainly as florist's flowers or for forcing. These include 'Paper White,' and 'Soleil d'Or.' The flowers are individually quite small, but produced in substantial numbers on top of tall stems. They cannot be considered as miniatures. But one or two forms have occurred which do come into this category.

N. tazetta subsp. bertolonii

N. tazette subsp. *aureus* is the wild form of 'Soleil d'Or,' and a small type has been found with bright yellow flowers on a 6–8 in. (15–20 cm) stem. This sounds splendid, but I have had bulbs for six years and have yet to see a flower. The bulbs grow well, split most rapidly, but that is all. I shall keep my pan so that perhaps one day I may see it flower, but a desirable bulb this certainly is not.

N. tazetta subsp. lacticolor (canaliculatus)

This is a true miniature *tazetta,* for the stem is not more than 4–5 in. (10–12.5 cm) tall with a cluster of small white flowers each with a small yellow cup. But again, it never blooms! Clearly there are different strains of this subspecies and I have two at the moment. The first splits into masses of small bulbs surmounted by a mat of fine foliage. The bulbs of the second are substantially larger, and I have had one or two flowers on these from time to time. But never more than one stem with perhaps three or four flowers in the truss. I have discarded the small-bulb type, and shall keep the larger form to see if I can make it bloom. But I see little future in either of these *tazetta* species. Neither is hardy outside in New Jersey.

N. dubius

This is presumed to be a natural hybrid between *N. tazetta* subsp. *papyraceus* and *N. requienii.* It is fertile, and readily crosses with other species and is also self-fertile. In effect it is a small and almost pure white *tazetta,* with the flower truss held on 4–5 in. (10–12.5 cm) stems. Because it is fertile this bulb has frequently been used for hybridizing. It does produce seed freely if self-pollinated, but the seed takes many years to reach flowering size, usually at least seven, if not more. It is an interesting bulb which grows without difficulty, and is of substantial potential as a breeding parent.

In addition to the above, I have bulbs of a reputed dwarf form of *N. tazetta* subsp. *italicus* var. *odoratus* but they have not bloomed. Until this year I had a dwarf *tazetta* collected in Sardinia. It flowered once, after which the main bulb rotted. This year it finally became extinct. There seems little future in either.

Narcissus dubius. A fine species to use for hybridizing.

Tazetta Hybrids

These are few in number, and with one or two exceptions those that we do have seem of little value.

'Angie'. Alec Gray. Camborne, England. 1948. 8 W-W. *N. dubius* × 'John Evelyn'.

I have not grown this cultivar and the few reports on it in literature suggest that it is a difficult bulb to grow.

'Cyclataz'. A. W. Tait. Portugal. 1923. 8 Y-O. *N. cyclamineus* × 'Soleil d'Or'.

It is not clear whether this cultivar arose from a planned cross or simply as a chance seedling in a garden in which both *N. cyclamineus* and many forms of *N. tazetta* were flowering. I doubt that the exact parentage has ever been determined, but, no matter, it is a nice bulb. Alec Gray considered it to be more of a cyclamineus type flower and so listed it in that section, but it is shown on the Approved List as a Division 8. Gray also states that this is the only hybrid he knows with 'Soleil d'Or' as one of the presumed parents. Accurate at that time, this is no longer true, for there

'Cyclataz'. Fine for pans but not hardy.

is at least one other hybrid which exists, this being a cross between 'Soleil d'Or' and *N. scaberulus.*

'Cyclataz' is a delightful bulb, producing stems not more than 6 in. (15 cm) high and with fresh, bright green foliage. The flower is a curious mixture, for there may be from two to four individual flowers on each stem, in the manner of 'Tete-a-Tete' and yet the petals on each flower tend to be reflexed backwards as in *N. cyclamineus.* It grows well, flowers in early February in pans, and seems to have no trouble with disease. In color it closely resembles 'Soleil d'Or' for the cup is orange and the petals yellow. It is an excellent pot plant, but may not be too hardy, and should not be planted out except in favored areas where other *tazetta* types can survive.

'Halingy'. Alec Gray. Camborne, England. 1949. 8 W-Y. 'Scilly White' × ?

Gray states that this was derived from 'Scilly White' and describes it as white with a pale yellow cup on 6 in. (15 cm) stems. I have had a pan of this cultivar now for four years without seeing a flower. This year it will be removed from the protection of the greenhouse and must do what it can in an unheated frame. It had better flower soon or it will be out altogether!

'Hors d' Oeuvre'. Alec Gray. Camborne, England. 1959. 8 Y-Y. *N. tazette* subsp. *lacticolor canaliculatus* × *N. minor.*

This cultivar has done very poorly for me. The only time that a flower was seen, it appeared to be a rather non-descript yellow on a 9 in. (22.8 cm) stem. I planted it outside and it disappeared.

'Minnow'. Best outdoors but also not too hardy.

'Minnow'. Alec Gray. Camborne, England. 1962. 8 W-Y. *N. tazetta* × ?

Unfortunately, Gray does not give the parentage of this very good cultivar. It is in fact the only really satisfactory Division 8 hybrid I have encountered. On stems 6 in. (15 cm) high, the flowers are a delightful creamy white with a bright yellow cup. A typical *tazetta* in habit, this is a very good bulb, although slightly tender outdoors in New Jersey. Because it is such a good bulb it is usually available from commercial suppliers as a Dutch import each fall.

'Pango'. Alec Gray. Camborne, England. 1949. 8 Y-W. *N. dubius* × 'John Evelyn'.

This is from the same cross as 'Angie' but the bulb appears to be a better grower, and is more generally available. Because it is on the tall side, 9 in. (22/9 cm), I have planted mine outside in a shaded and sheltered place near a large rhododendron, where it seems to do very well. The white flower is a very "smooth" one, with three to five flowers on a stem. The cup is a soft yellow. It tends to flower early and can be damaged by late frosts.

This brings us to the end of the Division 8 hybrids, and as can be seen, there is little from which to choose. Clearly, much more breeding needs to be done, probably using *N. dubius* as one of the parents.

N. poeticus

At this writing there are no really miniature wild species or subspecies among the Division 9, *N. poeticus,* nor are there any hybrids. *N. poeticus* subsp. *hellenicus* has

'Pango'. Will do outdoors if sheltered.

one of the smallest flowers in this section, and I understand that breeding is now going on to produce a true miniature 'poet.' However, none are as yet available commercially.

'Picoblanco'. Does well in pans.

CHAPTER TWELVE

Wild Hybrids and Odd Hybrids from Other Divisions

N. × macleayi. **10 W-Y.**

This form is considered to be a wild hybrid, although as far as I can learn, it has never been found growing in the wild. It is presumed to be a hybrid between *N. poeticus* and a form of *N. pseudonarcissus* although which one is not certain. Bowles records that it was first described in 1823 from a specimen sent to the Horticultural Society by Alexander Macleay, which he in turn had received from Smyrna. Although its origin is unclear, the plant is a good one and should be in any collection. In the last few years I have received a number of bulbs reputed to be *N. macleayi* but only this last year have I seen the correct plant. It is quite dwarf, with short but strong, broad, narcissus leaves. The size of the leaves belies the dwarfness of the scape, for this is usually not more than 6 in. (15 cm) high at the most, upon which is born a fairly large flower with white petals and a bright yellow cup. The cup in this instance is rather large, more of a trumpet than a cup. The bulb which finally flowered for me was growing outside and I have not yet tried it in pans.

We come finally to a short group of Division 3 hybrids which are included in the Approved List of Miniatures. With but one exception, I have considered all of these rather too tall for successful pan culture, but all are first class in the miniature border.

'X Tenuior'. **Origin unknown. 10 Y-Y.**

An extremely old bulb believed to be a natural hybrid between *N. jonquilla* and *N. poeticus,* although to the best of my knowledge, it has never been found in the wild. Clearly described in Curtis's Botanical Magazine in 1797, it is still being grown. I have had a bulb or two for some time but they have never done well. Last year I purchased three new bulbs. One was laced with stripe and was immediately discarded. The two remaining appeared superficially the same, yet distinct, for one had glaucus foliage and the other green. The green-leaved form had lax foliage, and when it flowered the petals were a muddy white, the dull yellow from the cup suffusing into the base of the petals. Although the stem was not more than 6 in. (15 cm) and the flower about 1 in. (2.5 cm) across, the effect was poor. The glaucus specimen had much stiffer foliage and a flower of pure white, with a distinct pale lemon-yellow cup. This was the better of the two, and so perhaps we may eventually establish a good form as a clone. However, it seems to be mainly of historical interest to the collector.

'Paula Cottell'. Alec Gray. Camborne, England. 1981. 3 W-WWY. 'Samaria' × ?

Gray does not give us the pollen parent, but this cultivar has a very smooth flower on a rather tall, 8–10 in. (20–25 cm) stem. It does very well for me in the garden. The white petals are broad, very well overlapped, and in the center is a small yellow cup. I use the adjective "smooth" advisedly, because this is the overall effect the bloom has. I like it—but outside.

'Picarillo'. Brian Mulligan. Seattle, Washington U.S.A. 1951. 2 Y-Y. *N. watieri* × *N. pseudonarcissus* var. *pumilus*.

Regretfully I have not grown this cultivar, but all speak well of it. It is at the top of my want list.

'Picoblanco'. Mrs. Alec Gray. Camborne, England. 1961. 3 W-W. *N. watieri* × ?

This cultivar is on the tall side, but I grow and enjoy it in pans nevertheless. The bulb is somewhat larger, and the foliage when mature of the normal narcissus type. The stems are 6 in. (15 cm) tall and the flowers of a clear, pure white. This is a "quality" flower on the same order as 'Snipe.' The bulb does well in pans and gives no trouble with disease.

'Segovia'. Mrs. Alec Gray. Camborne, England. 1962. 3 W-Y. *N. watieri* × ?

Although no parents are listed for this cultivar, one can assume, I think with reason, that it has to be a *N. watieri* cross. Rather on the tall side, I have it growing in the miniature border, where it does extremely well. A clump which has been down for some years now produces flowers in abundance each spring. The stems are perhaps 8–10 in. (20–25 cm) tall and the flowers are white, broad, flat, with a small yellow cup in the center. I find it rather difficult to differentiate between this form and the so-called 'Yellow Xit' for they seem very similar to me. I have grown 'Segovia' in pans but it is just too tall and lax to be attractive.

'Segovia'

'Xit'. Alec Gray. Camborne, England. 1948. 3 W-W. *N. watieri* × large Division 2.

Again the precise parentage is not given, but the bulb is clearly a *N. watieri* cross, being completely white. Gray calls for this to be 5–6 in. (12–15 cm) but it has always grown taller for me and so has been set out in the miniature border, where it does very well.

'Yellow Xit' Alec Gray. Camborne, England. 1968. 3 W-Y.

Confusion arose after 'Xit' was distributed because some bulbs flowered with a small yellow cup. This form was presumed to be a "sport" or mutation from the original and was registered twenty years later under this name. Apart from the difference in the cup they appear to be identical.

An Epilogue

To the best of my knowledge, this seems to be the end of the line, at least for the moment. For the line is, in reality, never at an end—there is always someone, somewhere, looking for something different, perhaps better, but certainly of interest to any keen horticulturalist.

In 1985 when the idea for this book came alive, I naturally approached Alec Gray to see if he had any objection to my attempting to bring his book up to date. The proposal was warmly received, followed by a suggestion that many notes which he had made during his active years might be of value. These had been deposited at Wisley and with his approval, were copied and sent to me. Now, sadly as I come to the end of my task, word of Alec Gray's passing comes, after a long and most rewarding life, at the age of 90. As you leaf through these pages, the name Alec Gray appears time and time again. There is no question that he, and he alone has been responsible for creating a class of daffodils which are unique and outstanding. Not satisfied to see and enjoy the daffodils for himself, he proceeded by every means available to lead others to appreciate them throughout the world.

It is given to very few to achieve such a sure place in horticultural history. There is no question that Alec Gray and his daffodils are certain to be remembered and appreciated for a very long time.

What lies ahead? Perhaps none of these delightful miniatures will achieve the pinnacle of acclaim accorded to some of the larger types. Yet there seems to be a small group of devotees who continue to cultivate and appreciate the qualities of delicacy and exquisite proportion found only in these truly miniature species and cultivars. And they seem to last, for their appeal is not affected by declining vigor, changing gardening tastes, or the arrival of superior cultivars which make them obsolete.

Consider if you will that our old friend 'King Alfred,' one of the larger daffodils, was registered in 1899 and for nearly three quarters of a century reigned supreme. But declining vigor and the introduction of better hybrids now places it in a well earned nitch in daffodil history. Then followed 'Fortune' in 1923, which enjoyed a premier place for more than 50 years, but is now on its decline as better bulbs appear.

Contrast this with the record of steady loyalty accorded the true miniatures over the centuries. The early appreciation of many of the jonquils has already been noted, but if you are fortunate enough to obtain a copy of *The Narcissus. Its History and Culture,* by F. W. Burbidge and J. G. Baker, published in 1875, therein you will see many fine colored plates of bulbs we enjoy today. Such bulbs as *N. bulbocodium* var. *monophyllus, N. triandrus* subsp. *calathinus* (now subsp. *capax*), and *N. pseudo-*

narcissus subsp. *moschatus* var. *alpestris* were then and remain today important elements of any good collection.

With so much in horticulture changing almost daily, such a degree of continuity and recognition is rare and should be treasured and enhanced in every possible way.

In July of 1986 I sent a substantial collection of miniatures to a grower who had become interested in them. Just 12 months later he could hardly stop talking about the many interests and pleasures which had unfolded for him through the winter. From September onwards his daffodil season had begun, increasing with each passing week as different species and hybrids came into flower, until by the end of the year he had a substantial display of bulbs which he had never previously known.

Then on through January and February and into March, when the usual outdoor season commenced, he could not have been more enthusiastic about his "wonderful winter daffodil season." He is interested in plants as well as ribbons, and it mattered not at all that many bulbs he enjoyed in mid-winter would never be seen on a show bench.

Help and encouragement has come from many people, beginning with Alec Gray who really was responsible for introducing me to these bulbs. Then followed generous help from John Blanchard who went out of his way to make available bulbs of extreme rarity and interest. Michael Salmon has added greatly to my list with some of his new collections. He continues to actively search land being devastated by developments in the natural bulb areas of Spain, Portugal and Morocco, rescuing plants from the advancing bulldozers. (Anyone interested in subscribing to one of his expeditions can contact him at Jacklands, Jacklands Bridge, Tickenham, Nr. Clevedon, Avon, England.) On one of my visits to him he showed me some of his splendid botanical illustrations of bulbs he had collected, and when asked, he readily agreed to produce the six plates which illustrate most of the important miniature narcissus species. I feel most fortunate to have these as part of this book, for they will ensure the continued value of the book to future enthusiasts.

Henning Christian in Portugal never forgets to gather a few bulbs for me when he is roaming the hills. Many others have exchanged bulbs and I thank them all, for without this free exchange I would not have the collection recorded here. Mrs. Paul Gripshover, until recently the editor of the American Daffodil Society's Journal, was most helpful in reading my early drafts, and trying to keep me on the right path. Finally, I am deeply indebted to Christopher Brickell, Director General of The Royal Horticultural Society, who kindly undertook the onerous task of checking and correcting my botanical structure and names. Although he has done this with great care, there may be some omissions and possibly mistakes here which, if found, are my responsibility only.

I commenced this manuscript with the idea that it would be an updated version of Alec Gray's book, now long out of print. I hope that this has been accomplished at least to some degree but, as Gray found when he finished his writing, what is put down inevitably becomes a somewhat personal account of what one thinks and what one has done. But I hope that in the essentials I have been able to open the door a little wider to an area of horticulture which to the typical gardener might not be immediately apparent.

So if this book has a purpose, over and above trying to bring information up to date, it is the hope that your horticultural horizons will be widened as you read. You may become interested in growing and enjoying this special group of plants which have been appreciated and passed down for many generations. Thus you might become another link in the chain that joins us all to both the past and the future.

APPENDIX A

An International Standard Collection of Narcissus Species and Miniature Hybrids

In todays world every significant undertaking has to establish a recognized set of standards. The American Daffodil Society recognized this requirement in establishing the Approved List of Miniatures. But there remains a wide gap between the list and reality; the reality is that in many instances one really does not know what is correct, what is true. It would be reassuring for example if we could order from every source with confidence that we would receive correct and true bulbs. But although some growers are much better than others, the problem of keeping these very small bulbs straight is a difficult matter. There are wide differences in forms among the species supplied under the same label, presumably due to collections being made in the wild by different people at different times.

Clearly there is a need for a standard collection, established and maintained in a well-run horticultural center, where the bulbs will receive the careful and individual attention many of them require to become established and develop their full potential. This is particularly true of the species.

Such an undertaking in turn requires a high level of botanical knowledge, and an organization devoted to providing the detailed care required to ensure the proper development of the collection. Some guarantee of continuity is essential, so that the collection can be assured of years of high-level care.

As far as I know, there is no such collection of miniature daffodils in existence yet. But those who have been to England in the spring and seen the natural display of species growing with abandon in the lawns of both The Savill Gardens and Wisley know how well they do there.

It occurred to me some time ago that The Savill Gardens was just the place to establish such a collection, and I am pleased to report that the suggestion met with immediate approval. A fair collection is already growing there, but what is needed now is the world-wide support of miniature daffodil growers. If every grower, commercial or amateur, would send a bulb of this or that which can be spared, so that the forms could be compared, the objective of the enterprise would quickly be realized. The final aim is to establish a permanent collection which will be available to anyone as a guide.

This concept urgently needs your help, and I hope that all those who read this book will set about sorting out a few surplus bulbs and send them to The Keeper of the Garden at the Savill Gardens. Do not worry about duplications, as they are necessary and desirable for comparison and final judging.

The shipping of bulbs is very simple. Bulbs should be clean, dry and free of soil. Put them in a paper bag—NOT PLASTIC—together with a label, separate bags for each species or cultivar.

A health certificate is desirable if available. This can usually be obtained from your local horticultural extension agent without difficulty and without cost. Mail at once in a small padded mailer and BY AIR MAIL, small package to:

> The Keeper of the Garden
> The Crown Estate Office
> The Great Park. Windsor. Berks. SL4 2HT ENGLAND

This is a wonderful chance to invest in the future.

APPENDIX B

A Glossary of Botanical Terms Used in the Text

Anther. The upper portion of a stamen which contains the pollen.

Clone. Identical, asexually produced progeny.

Corona. The cup, trumpet-shaped or disc-like outgrowth in the center of the flower.

Crenulated. Finely scalloped.

Cultivar. A cultivated variety, sexually or asexually produced and more or less uniform in character.

Exserted. Projecting

Filament. The stalk supporting an anther.

Filiform. Slender, rounded, and thread-shaped.

Glaucus. A light, bluish-gray color.

Lax. Loose and or scattered.

Morphology. The form and structure of plants.

Mutant. A plant changed by mutation, i.e. spontaneously.

Nematocide. A chemical capable of destroying nematodes.

Nomenclature. A system of terms—as in the naming of plants.

Ovary. The immature seed vessel.

Parthenocarpic. The production of seeds or fruits without fertilization.

Pedicel. The stalk of a single flower.

Perianth. The colored, floral leaves, composed of sepals and petals.

Perianth Segment. One of the floral leaves of the perianth.

Perianth Tube. The hollow, cylindrical or funnel-shaped portion of the flower between the ovary and the segments.

Pistil. The female organ, consisting of ovary, style and stigma.

Reflexed. Turned or directed backwards.

Scape. A leafless flower stalk.

Serrated. Notched or toothed on the edge.

Sessile. Without a stalk.

Stamen. The male organ, consisting of anther and filament.

Stigma. The upper part of the pistil which receives the pollen.

Style. The lower, slender part of the pistil which bears the stigma at its apex.

Strain. A selected stock of a cultivar which breeds true from seed.

Taxonomy. Botanic classification system.

APPENDIX C

Alphabetical Index to Species and Cultivars, with Indications as to Their Best Use

APPENDIX D

Bibliography

The American Daffodil Society. *The Daffodil Journal* 1971–1987.

The American Daffodil Society. *Daffodils To Show and Grow.* 1980.

The American Daffodil Society. *Miniature Species and Cultivars* 1987. Computer printout.

American Horticultural Society. *The Daffodil Handbook* 1966.

Baker, J. G. and Burbridge, F. W. *The Narcissus. Its History and Culture.* 1875.

Barr, P. *Ye Narcissus or Daffodyl Flower and Hys Roots* 1884.

Bowles, E. A. *A Handbook of Narcissus.* 1934. Martin Hopkinson.

Calvert, A. F. *Daffodil Growing for Pleasure and Profit* 1929. Dulau.

Fernandez, A. "Key to the identification of native and naturalized taxa of the genes narcissus." *R. H. S. Daffodil Yearbook.* 1968.

Flora Europaea. Volume 5. 1980.

Gray, Alec. *Miniature Daffodils.* 1955. Collingridge.

Gray-Wilson, C. and Mathew B. *The Bulbous Plants of Europe and Their Allies.* 1981.

Gould, Charles J. *Diseases of Narcissus.* Extension Bulletin #709, Washington State University. Pullman, WA. 99164.

Jefferson-Brown, M. *The Daffodil.* 1951. Faber & Faber.

Mathew Brian. *Dwarf Bulbs.* 1973.

Royal Horticultural Society. *Daffodil Yearbook* 1933–1987.

Royal Horticultural Society. *Classified List and International Register of Daffodil Names.* 1969.

Rix, Martyn. and Phillips, Roger. *The Bulb Book.* 1981.

Salmon. Michael. *Narcissus in North Africa.* R.H.S. Daffodil Yearbook 1986–87.

Snazelle, Dr. Theodore. *Daffodil Diseases and Pests.* 1986.

Synge, P. *The Collins Guide to Bulbs.* 1961.

Index to Plant Names

Note: page numbers in roman type indicate text references; page numbers in italics indicate illustration. Cultivars are listed first, followed by *Narcissus* entries.